Pilgrimage

Pilgrimage

MY JOURNEY TO A DEEPER FAITH IN THE LAND WHERE JESUS WALKED

LYNN AUSTIN

BETHANYHOUSE

a division of Baker Publishing Group
Minneapolis, Minnesota

Published by Bethany House Publishers
11400 Hampshire Avenue South
Bloomington, Minnesota 55438
www.bethanyhouse.com

Bethany House Publishers is a division of
Baker Publishing Group, Grand Rapids, Michigan

Printed in the United States of America

Library of Congress Cataloging-in-Publication Data is on file at the Library of Congress, Washington, DC.

ISBN 978-0-7642-1118-8 (pbk.)

Unless otherwise indicated, Scripture quotations are taken from the HOLY BIBLE, NEW INTERNATIONAL VERSION®. Copyright © 1973, 1978, 1984 Biblica. Used by permission of Zondervan. All rights reserved.

Scripture quotations identified as KJV are from the King James Version of the Bible.

Scripture quotations identified as THE MESSAGE are from *The Message* by Eugene H. Peterson, copyright © 1993, 1994, 1995, 2000, 2001, 2002. Used by permission of NavPress Publishing Group. All rights reserved.

Cover design by Jennifer Parker
Cover imagery by Inspirestock Inc. / Alamy

Holy Land photo by Lynn Austin

Interior illustrations by Louise Bass. Used by permission.

13   14   15   16   17   18   19   7   6   5   4   3   2   1

To my dear friends and fellow writers
Jane Rubietta and Cleo Lampos

And to my faithful friend and
cheerleader Cathy Pruim

CONTENTS

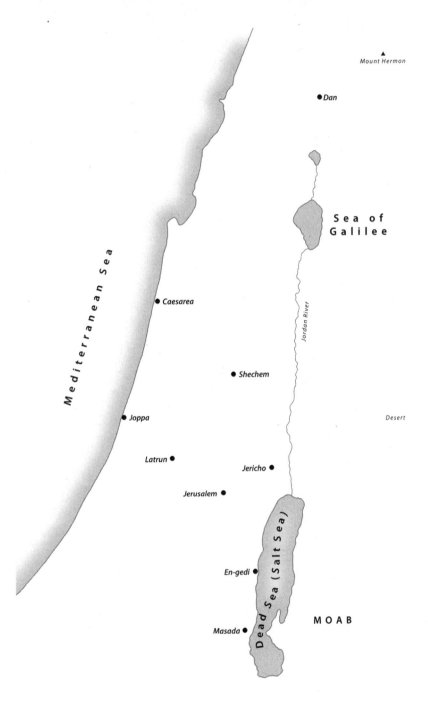

Mount Hermon

• Dan

Sea of
Galilee

Mediterranean Sea

• Caesarea

Jordan River

• Shechem

Desert

• Joppa

Latrun •

Jericho •

Jerusalem •

Dead Sea (Salt Sea)

En-gedi •

MOAB

Masada •

WILDERNESS of ZIN

1

LEAVING HOME
AND HO-HUM

I rejoiced with those who said to me, "Let us go to the house
of the Lord." Our feet are standing in your gates, O Jerusalem.

Psalm 122:1–2

My journey to Israel has been long and wearying. I
feel like a bedraggled contestant on a TV reality
show as I near the end. I've endured two airplane
flights totaling twelve hours—hours spent sitting, standing,
rushing through airport corridors, hauling bags and pass-
ports and suitcases. They were confusing, jet-lagged hours
when I didn't know if it was day or night as I tried to wedge
myself into a cramped airplane seat and sleep. At some point
during the night, I wandered lost through Heathrow Airport
during a stopover in London. I have run the hectic obstacle
course of airport security three times and waited in endless
lines, the final one here in Israel's Ben Gurion Airport where

the no-nonsense passport inspectors wear pistols. The journey has been a parody of my life recently: rushing, waiting, wandering, feeling lost and losing sleep, wondering if I'm getting anywhere.

But at last I pull my limping luggage through the airport doors to claim my prize. And what a prize it is! Palm trees rustle and sway in welcome. The warm evening air smells of sweet spices and green earth. I've arrived in time to watch the setting sun gild the Israeli sky before it disappears into the Mediterranean Sea. Something inside me releases a sigh. A tangled knot in my soul relaxes and begins to unwind. I have arrived in the land where Jesus walked. My pilgrimage has begun.

The opportunity to tour Israel came at a good time. For months, my life has been a mindless plodding through necessary routine, as monotonous as an all-night shift on an assembly line. Life gets that way sometimes, when nothing specific is wrong but the world around us seems drained of color. Even my weekly worship experiences and daily quiet times with God have felt dry and stale. I'm ashamed to confess the malaise I've felt. I have been given so much. Shouldn't a Christian's life be an abundant one, as exciting as Christmas morning, as joyful as Easter Sunday?

I have to wait a few minutes for our tour bus to arrive, so I drop my suitcase near the curb and shrug off my carry-on bag, aware of the symbolism of laying my burdens down. It feels good to walk a bit and stretch my legs. In twelve hours I've gone from snow to sand, from bare trees to palm trees, from biting cold to merciful warmth. I needed a change, and I welcome these. But back home, too many changes—unwelcome and unexpected—had erupted in my life like dormant volcanoes, rumbling and smoking and creating havoc.

Within five months, all three of our adult children moved far away from home, leaving our nest permanently empty for the first time. Our older son and his wife found new jobs in another state. They no longer attend the same church we do, share a pew with us, join us for Sunday dinner. I feel their absence like a pulled tooth, and I can't stop probing that still-tender spot, surprised by the pain and the hole they've left behind. I had imagined that they would always live nearby, where I could watch my grandchildren grow up and be part of their lives. My imagination is the problem, you see, especially when it collides with God's plan for my life and the lives of my children.

Our younger son has moved to Europe for four years to study for his doctoral degree in Biblical Studies. I'm proud of

Tower of David

11

him and excited about what God has for his future, but that doesn't stop me from missing him. The move also forced me to acknowledge that his intended career as a Bible professor and theologian would likely keep him far away on a permanent basis. In fact, one of his goals after he completes his studies is to teach at a seminary in a third-world country, helping to train local pastors and leaders. Again, my dream of having my extended family nearby will be sacrificed to God's plans. Why couldn't He call my son to live next door and teach in a seminary nearby?

Our only daughter left her job and her apartment close to home and has moved here to Israel to study. How could I welcome such a change, watching my youngest child set off all alone to live in a land that is the constant target of terrorists, enemy missiles, and suicide bombers? When she was fourteen years old she visited Israel with my husband and me and fell in love with this land. Afterward, she befriended several Jewish schoolmates and their families. "I think God is calling me to a ministry with the Jewish people," she said after hearing a sermon on discovering God's will for her life. In my heart I hoped she was mistaken, that it was a case of youthful exuberance. But time has proven that her call was from God, and now, after she completes her studies here in Israel, she plans to stay here, live here, work here. It helps to know that she is in the will of God—the safest place to be. But it doesn't stop me from worrying about her and missing her. I will see her on this trip, even though our visit will be brief.

There have been other losses in my life, as well. My sister Bonnie, my dearest, lifelong friend, died of cancer. My husband's brother and one of his sisters also died recently, leaving empty places in my heart and life. I can no longer call them on the phone or sit and visit over coffee. A dull physical pain has settled on my chest as I've confronted these losses, mimicking the deep, emotional ache my children's absence leaves inside me, as if an important part of me has been hollowed out. I think I'm a little angry with God because things haven't turned out the way I always pictured them. Depression, I've learned, is sometimes caused by anger that we keep locked up inside. Was this why I've felt so ambivalent about going to church? Why my daily devotions are as gray and limp and lifeless as a soggy tissue? Why my prayers have become a dull routine? I've wanted my will, not God's. But what is His will for me in all these changes?

On the outside, I'm in the same place that I have always been, pursuing the same calling of writing Christian fiction. But inside, I sometimes feel so disoriented that I think I've exchanged my life on land for life in a sailboat on the high seas—and I don't know how to sail. I don't even know how to swim.

I have experienced similar spiritual upheavals at other times in my life, times when the Scriptures were just words on a page and my prayers failed to lift off, grounded by a thick cloud of doubt. Each time, God has taught me some important lessons after I made up my mind to dig in and search for Him with all my heart. The lessons were life-changing—there's that dreaded *change* word again—but they brought me closer to God.

During one of those desert times as I wrestled with unanswered prayer, wondering why God was silent in the face of suffering, I came across a novel called *The Chosen* by Jewish author Chaim Potok. It's the story of the relationship between a father and his son, and what happens when the father makes the radical decision to raise his son in silence. Not as a punishment, as the story eventually reveals, but as an act of love for the son's ultimate benefit. In this novel, I saw a picture of Father God and His sometimes inexplicable silences. It enabled me to look beyond my own unanswered prayers and see God's love.

But the book did much more than open my eyes. It inspired me to consider writing fiction, taking readers into the world of Christianity the same way that Chaim Potok had taken me into the world of Orthodox Judaism. Christian fiction was in its infancy back then, but I felt a calling to write novels that would touch readers' hearts with Christ's love. Without that dry time in my life and my wrestling match with God, who knows if I would be writing fiction today?

So, yes, I understand that God might want to set me adrift on the high seas to shock me out of my complacency. I've decided to accept the churning waves as an invitation from God to draw closer to Him, to dig deeper into His Word, to seek Him with all my heart and soul and strength. Most of all, to begin to pray to Him in a better way. Perhaps I will find a compass or a book of sailing instructions, or at least a life preserver. Maybe, just maybe, this pilgrimage to Israel will get me started on that new journey.

I will be in good company on my trip. God commanded the Israelites to make pilgrimages to Jerusalem three times a year for the three annual religious festivals of Passover, Pentecost, and Tabernacles. Did they feel the same way I do as they began their journey: tired from slogging through the same old routines, worried about their children and families, battered by unexpected changes? Who has time to give more than a fleeting thought to God when life gets hard? But three times a year the Israelites had to pause in their labor and put aside their daily tasks as an act of faith and make a pilgrimage to Jerusalem.

I can see God's wisdom in making it a command. Otherwise, like most of us, they never would have found time to shoehorn God into their crowded lives. Excuses take over. We're much too busy. Most of us have such long to-do lists that even the Sabbath, the day He ordained for us to stop working and worship Him, is hardly a day of rest. God knows human nature, and unless He commanded it, His people never would have taken time off to worship. But worship helps us recognize our need for God. During these three yearly festivals, Israel remembered what God had done for them and reenacted the history of their salvation. They left behind their routine lives to celebrate God's goodness and renew their faith so they could return home refreshed and reconnected with the God who walked with them every day.

Spiritual renewal is what I long for, too, as I begin this pilgrimage. I want to see the bigger picture of His plan and learn to accept His will in all things. I want to revitalize my prayer life, really listening to what He is saying to me and asking His help through these changes. Maybe I'll be able to let go of my own will and face the changes in my life with joy and faith. That's asking a lot for a two-week trip. But this is Israel—the stage on which the Old and New Testaments are set, a land where Scripture springs to life in three dimensions like a children's pop-up book. Old friends from the Bible's pages populate these sites, and the words of patriarchs and prophets take on new significance as I gaze at the same rivers and mountains and lakes and deserts that they once viewed. In the landscape of Israel, I can visualize Jesus' parables and teachings because the cues are all around me—sheep and rocks and city walls and olive trees. Each site I visit is a rich layer cake of history with archaeological ruins dating not only to the time of Christ, but all the way back to Abraham's time. Since I will be "surrounded by such a great cloud of witnesses," maybe—just maybe—by journey's end I will be ready to "run with perseverance the race marked out" for me (Hebrews 12:1).

The tour bus has arrived, and the driver loads our luggage as our guide and my husband wait. I want to linger in the fading, golden light a moment longer, yet I'm eager to begin. We will start in the south—the Negev—then travel up through the central hill country to Jerusalem, and finally to the region of Galilee in the north. I will be exploring the land from south to north, the opposite way that Abraham explored it when he arrived in the Promised Land four thousand years ago. But it's the direction that the Israelites traveled as they left behind a life of slavery in Egypt, ended their aimless desert wanderings, and arrived at last to reclaim their homeland and worship their God.

And so my journey begins in the Negev . . .

The Lord had said to Abram, "Leave your country, your people and your father's household and go to the land I will show you." . . . So Abram left, as the Lord had told him . . . Abram traveled through the land as far as the site of the great tree of Moreh at Shechem . . . From there he went on toward the hills east of Bethel . . . Then Abram set out and continued toward the Negev.

Genesis 12:1, 4, 6, 8–9

A NEW PRAYER FOR THE JOURNEY

Heavenly Father,

I praise You for Your vast, unending love, as high and wide as the skies I have just flown through. I confess that I have behaved like a whining child, ignoring all of the ways You have provided for me as a loving parent and complaining instead, wanting my own way, my own plans. Forgive me for allowing disappointment and loss to hinder my prayers and my relationship with You. Stand me on my feet again, Lord, and teach me how to walk on the paths You have chosen for me. Help me to accept Your comfort for my losses and Your will for the changes in my life. Teach me how to pray on this journey in a new and better way so that I can draw closer to You, the Source of all good things. Thank You for the new beginning we have in Christ Jesus and for this new beginning in my life.

Amen

2

THE WILDERNESS OF ZIN

O God, you are my God, earnestly I seek you; my soul thirsts
for you, my body longs for you, in a dry and weary land
where there is no water.

Psalm 63:1

The sun blazes overhead in a cloudless sky. The expanse of dry, trackless land all around me resembles the surface of the moon. There are no boundaries in this wasteland, no landmarks on the barren earth, nothing but rocks and dirt and inhospitable peaks stretching to the horizon in every direction. Sweat rolls down my face and the back of my shirt. I guzzle water like a cartoon character.

My pilgrimage in Israel has begun in the Wilderness of Zin, a vast stretch of colorless desert south of Beersheba and the Dead Sea. The bleak scenery mirrors the state of my soul: parched and lifeless. Only a fool would venture into this wilderness without a water supply and a guide who knows the way. No fool, I'm carrying two water bottles that slosh like lapping bloodhounds as I walk. And since I can barely discern the path we're on from the rest of our surroundings, I stick very close to our tour guide. I follow him in faith, trusting that he knows the way.

After two hours of vigorous hiking with no end in sight, I have a newfound empathy for the Israelites, condemned by their unbelief to wander for forty years in this wilderness. I picture them plodding forward, one foot in front of the other, as hot and miserable as I am. But unlike me, the Israelites carried goat-hair tents and heavy clay cooking pots and bedding for the freezing nighttime temperatures. And they had their children with them—hordes of weary, whining children. No wonder Israel's murmuring against Moses grew louder and louder: "Was it because there were no graves in Egypt that you have brought us to the desert to die? . . . It would have been better for us to serve the Egyptians than to die in the desert!" (Exodus 14:11–12). I now understand their complaint from firsthand experience. I will be hiking here for only a few days; any longer and I might prefer a life of slavery, too.

I wonder if the fear and aversion we feel in these desert places spring from the fact that God created us to live in a garden. He provided everything we needed in lush, fertile Eden: water, food, and unhindered communion with Him. Out here, with no visible source of food or water, no shelter from the elements, it's easy to succumb to the fear that we've been abandoned by God in this desolate place. Maybe that's why we call the dry, parched times in our lives, when our soul withers and God seems very far away, "a wilderness experience."

Such experiences often come at times of change and upheaval. When God wants to shake us free from our old habits and lead us into a new walk with Him, He sometimes begins with a desert journey. The Israelites left a life of slavery—and the leeks and melons and cucumbers of Egypt—and began their new life of freedom here in the desert. And even the modern nation of Israel began in the desert at the time of its founding in 1948. More than half of the acreage allotted to the Jews by the United Nations' partition was in wilderness areas like this one. For bewildered immigrants from the Holocaust-torn cities of Europe, this vast emptiness where I'm now walking must have seemed like a strange new beginning. Talk about adapting to change!

God knows that we all need to be brought out to the desert from time to time to free us from our comfortable self-sufficiency. If He strips us of all our own resources, we just might learn to lean on Him. And to start praying again. With the luxuries of Egypt far behind them, Moses and the Israelites had no choice but to trust God, who graciously provided unlimited manna to feed them and fresh water from a rock to quench their thirst. The desert journey was supposed to build their faith for the years ahead when they would have to face enemies and conquer the Promised Land. If God could protect and sustain them here, they could trust Him anywhere. Maybe that's what this desert time in my own life is supposed to accomplish. Maybe God wants me to stop grumbling and looking back at the past and learn to trust Him for my future.

The truth is, I really don't want to walk by faith. Do any of us? I prefer comfort and safety, a well-stocked pantry and an abundant water supply, a map that shows exactly where I'm going and how long it will take to get there—and I would like to choose the destination myself, thank you. But who needs God if I have all those things? Israel's downfall didn't come when they were homeless wanderers in the desert, but when they lived in cities where they were self-sufficient and well fed. God had warned them that, "When you eat and are satisfied, when you build fine houses and settle down . . . then your heart will become proud and you will forget the Lord your God, who . . . led you through the vast and dreadful desert, that thirsty and waterless land" (Deuteronomy 8:12, 14–15). God must have known that I needed this walk beneath the relentless sun, through this dry, empty wasteland to remind me of my need for Him.

The sun has reached its peak and is beginning its descent toward the western horizon. My last water bottle is nearly empty. We have been hiking for miles with no idea where we are, trusting the guide to lead us out of here. I don't think I can walk much farther. When I look ahead and see that our path is about to end at the foot of an imposing mountain ridge, towering above us, I want to sit down and cry. Will we have to retrace our steps through all those long, wearying miles in the barren desert? Our guide continues forward, straight toward the base of the cliff. The only way out appears to be straight up. Impossible.

We soon reach the dead end and sink down to rest on the bare ground, weary and discouraged. It wouldn't take much for us to start hurling stones at our guide. But after letting us catch our breath, he prods us to our feet—and shows us a nearly invisible, hand-hewn staircase cut into the side of the cliff, complete with iron handholds. I think I know how the parched Israelites felt when Moses struck the barren rock with his staff and water miraculously gushed out. I follow the guide up the treacherous cliff, one careful footstep at a time.

At last I reach the top, breathless from the climb, and see our air-conditioned tour bus waiting for us. As the other hikers snap photographs from this dizzying height, I wander off alone and savor the panoramic view of endless wilderness all around me. I remember the long, long way I have come. There is a beauty in this formidable place that I wouldn't have wanted to miss. The wilderness has given me a sense of my own frailty and of my need for God. He seems very near to me now as I stand alone in the stark, pristine silence. Before today, I thought I faced a dead end in my life. But even though the path may still be hidden from my sight, even though the climb may be steep and treacherous, God truly does know the way.

It's time to board the bus and be refreshed by the cool air. I sink into my seat for a much-deserved rest. I still face frightening changes and challenges back home, but I no longer fear the wilderness. It's where I will learn, all over again, to trust God.

Helpless

After a bountiful meal and a good night's rest, we're hiking once again in the wilderness areas of southern Israel. Today we'll explore the Ramon Crater, a smaller version of America's Grand Canyon, but no less beautiful or awe-inspiring. We begin at the canyon's rim, gazing down at the jagged slit in the earth's crust, twenty-five miles long and five miles wide. I'm told that the rainbow layers of rock and dirt and sediment are a geologist's paradise, complete with prehistoric fossils and the remnants of an extinct volcano. The desolate, reddish-gold landscape is how I picture the surface of Mars—lifeless. But our guide assures us that this area is a nature reserve, home to wild ibex, gazelles, hyenas, and an animal I don't wish to meet along the trail—leopards. We take photographs from this vantage point, inhale the clean desert air, enjoy the surprising breeze, and then board the bus to our hiking trail along the canyon's bottom, five hundred feet below.

Soon I'm trekking through an alien landscape like something from a cheap science fiction film. The deeper we walk into the canyon and the farther we go from the bus, the more aware I become of my utter helplessness. I can't build a shelter to escape from the heat in a place without trees. We've been warned that scorpions and vipers make their homes among the rocks. What appears to be an oasis is often a mirage. There is no place to turn to for help—and the emptiness goes on and on with no end in sight. All of my self-sufficiency vanishes in this hostile, unforgiving place.

Before leaving my hotel room this morning, I read Psalm 63—"A psalm of David when he was in the Desert of Judah." David spent years living in desolate places like this while hiding from his enemy King Saul. How did he survive the doubt and discouragement he must have felt, the terrifying helplessness?

The psalm begins, "O God, you are my God, earnestly I seek you; my soul thirsts for you, my body longs for you, in a dry and weary land where there is no water" (v. 1). In other words, David was in a spiritual wilderness as well as a physical one. I imagine him walking a desolate trail like this one, hot and weary and discouraged, knowing that on the other side of the hill, Saul's army is encamped with their weapons and provisions and water supplies. To David, the day that the prophet Samuel poured oil on his head and anointed him as Israel's king must have seemed like a fading dream, as disappointing as a mirage. How easy it is to doubt God's promises when we're weary and thirsty and afraid.

David combats his feelings of helplessness by looking back and remembering what he knows about God: "I have seen you in the sanctuary and beheld your power and your glory" (v. 2). He recalls God's great love for him, and even if David's current circumstances seem as hopeless as this wasteland all around him, he doesn't trust what he sees. It's a mirage. God's promises are the reality, and so David confidently says, "They who seek my life will be destroyed" (v. 9).

We know the end of the story—Saul and his armies were destroyed and David became king—so it's easy to forget that when David wrote those words, he didn't know if he would survive the desert, let alone become king of Israel. But he chose to trust God, and I can do the same. Instead of focusing on my current circumstances, I can look back and remember what I know about God, about how far He has brought me in this journey. I can recall His goodness and faithfulness to me in the past, the storms and dry places He has carried me through. I can look up into the endless desert sky and trust His love for me, "For as high as the heavens are above the earth, so great is his love for those who fear him" (Psalm 103:11). David trusted that his time in the desert would end one day, and so would his spiritual drought: "My soul will be satisfied as with the richest of foods," he wrote. "I sing in the shadow of your wings" (Psalm 63:5, 7).

A group of students hiking ahead of me begins to sing. I hear my husband's laughter behind me, and I remember that David wasn't alone in the desert. He not only felt God's presence with him, but he also had flesh-and-blood companions: "All those who were in distress or in debt or discontented gathered around him, and he became their leader" (1 Samuel 22:2). *Distressed* and *discontented*? Yikes! That's hardly the company I would choose! I've been with disgruntled, self-pitying complainers in the past, and I couldn't wait to leave them. Unhappiness can be as contagious as chicken pox. Grumblers nibble away at hope like a child eats candy. But God gave those four hundred discontented men to David to be his companions. They endured years of hardship with him in this treacherous place, and when David finally became king, they shared his triumph, as well.

Comfort also came from David's close friend Jonathan, the son of David's enemy King Saul. "While David was at Horesh in the Desert of Ziph . . . Saul's son Jonathan went to David . . . and helped him find strength in God" (1 Samuel 23:15–16). That's the kind of friend we need in our wilderness times—like a dear friend of mine who once dropped everything to sit in the hospital waiting room and pray with

Burnt House

me when my husband underwent emergency surgery. It's the kind of friend I should be to someone else.

So often I have felt alone in my journey, yet I've been afraid to let anyone see my fear and weakness. What would they think of me? Someone who has been a Christian for as long as I have shouldn't feel afraid or discouraged. As in the words of the children's song, shouldn't we be "happy, happy, happy all the time"? Again, I look at King David's example. He was a powerful warrior who had faced a giant single-handedly, yet he wasn't afraid to turn to his friends for strength or to ask for help in fighting his battles. Why do I try to be so independent, facing discouragement and change and loss all alone? Why am I too proud to ask for prayer? Even Jesus asked His friends to pray with Him in Gethsemane.

I turn and look behind me and see a college student from our group hiking all alone, plodding dispiritedly, sweating and red-faced. I slow down and wait for her to catch up to me. Her water bottles are empty, so I offer her a drink from mine. "Where are you from?" I ask her. "What are you studying in school?" As I listen, I forget about my own aching feet and weary body for a while, and I think she feels better, too.

The wilderness is a place where we can lean on God and trust His promises, but it's also a place to discover that the arms He provides and the ears that listen to our fears sometimes belong to flesh-and-blood people. Instead of carrying my discouragement alone, I need to accept help and then offer help in return. Like David's distressed and discontented companions, the people God sends my way might be just as weary and fearful of the future as I am. Maybe together, praying for each other, bearing one another's burdens, the journey will be lighter for all of us.

Falling Stars

We are nearly to the end of the trail. I am looking up, marveling at the beautiful, cloudless desert sky, when I happen to see a shooting star streaking across the heavens from horizon to horizon. "Did you see that?" I ask my husband. "I just saw a falling star!"

He stares at me as if I'm crazy. "Lynn, you can't see stars—it's broad daylight." It takes me a moment to realize what I have just seen. A missile! We are, after all, in Israel, a nation continually on the alert for enemy attacks.

This tiny country the size of New Jersey has been surrounded and outnumbered by enemies since its founding. Its territory covers only 8,000 square miles, while more than 5 million square miles of land belong to the surrounding Muslim nations. And Israel's population of 7 million is tiny compared to its neighbors' combined populations of 330 million. No wonder we've seen Israeli fighter jets patrolling the skies every day, watching from above. Once or twice, I've jumped in surprise when a jet has broken the sound barrier with an explosive sonic boom.

Our bus has traveled through military checkpoints manned by unsmiling, well-armed soldiers. We've seen barbed wire security fences and protective walls and signs that warn about the danger of buried land mines. We have passed through metal detectors on our way into restaurants and shopping malls and had our purses and backpacks searched. And it is commonplace to see teenage Israeli soldiers munching French fries at McDonald's with rifles strapped to their backs. Yes, Israel is very much aware of her enemies. Yet I feel completely safe here. The price of freedom, someone once said, is eternal vigilance.

At the moment I'm not aware of any enemies stalking me out here in the desert—except thirst or weariness, perhaps. But I recall from Scripture that enemies often choose wilderness places such as this no-man's-land to launch their attacks. Moses led the Israelites only a short distance from Egypt when Pharaoh and his armies came thundering after them in chariots, their swords and spears gleaming. Further down the road, before the weary Israelites could reach their destination at Mount Sinai, the Amalekites launched a surprise attack. And where did Jesus face temptation from His adversary, Satan? In the wilderness.

Enemies like to take advantage of our disorientation and vulnerability to sneak up on us, ambushing us when we're lost and weak. Like predators in a wildlife documentary, our enemies always go after the stragglers, the young, the feeble. The assault is even more horrifying if we're not expecting it. Remember our shock at the 9/11 attacks? We discovered that day that we had enemies we weren't even aware of. For months afterward, Americans were told to remain vigilant, watching for suspicious persons and activity. And then we grew complacent, trusting that the Department of Homeland Security was doing its job.

The missile that just flamed across the sky has jolted me from my slumber. I have been in a desert place for months, spiritually weakened and vulnerable to enemy attacks, yet I have not been vigilant. Seeing Israel's constant state of readiness reminds me that as a citizen in the kingdom of God, I will always be at war until Jesus returns. "Be self-controlled and alert. Your enemy the devil prowls around like a roaring lion looking for someone to devour" (1 Peter 5:8). And the devil isn't my only enemy. The attractions that the world offers, along with my own human desires and fears, conspire to lure me away from God's path. The depression and inertia I've felt lately is probably the result of such an assault. I have allowed the enemy to rob me of my greatest weapon—joy. And "the joy of the Lord is your strength" (Nehemiah 8:10).

When the Philippian Christians were under enemy attack, the Apostle Paul wrote to them saying, "Rejoice in the Lord always. I will say it again: Rejoice!" (Philippians 4:4). Beaten and chained in prison, Paul and Silas sang praises to God. And for all three of Israel's annual pilgrimage festivals, the people of God were told to "rejoice before the Lord your God, you, your sons and daughters, your menservants and maidservants" (Deuteronomy 12:12). Joy explodes throughout the book of Psalms like fireworks and is the most potent antimissile defense system there is.

Besides re-arming myself with joy, I need to know the holes in my defenses, the places where I'm vulnerable and where the enemy has successfully attacked me before. One of my greatest areas of weakness is worry. I can fret over a problem obsessively, rehearsing arguments and counterarguments, wasting days at a time in nonproductive stewing. Most of the things I worry about never happen. I need to develop a defensive strategy to combat worry, such as keeping a prayer journal and rereading it when I'm under attack. It will remind me of all the ways that God has taken care of my worries in the past, answering my prayers in ways I could never imagine. The price of freedom from worry and fear is eternal vigilance.

The young Israeli soldiers who carry their guns with them everywhere they go display this vigilance. Back home, no one walks around my community fully armed except the police. But once I understand that my enemy is never going to lay down arms and sign a peace treaty with me, I would be wise to remain on full alert at all times. "Put on the full armor of God so you can take your stand against the devil's schemes," Paul warned the Christians in Ephesus (Ephesians 6:11). Jesus used a piece of that armor, "the belt of truth," when He was in the wilderness, countering Satan's lies with truth from God's Word. And when His disciples rejoiced that even the demons had submitted to them in Jesus' name, He replied, "I saw Satan fall like lightning from heaven" (Luke 10:18). Bam! A successful anti-missile strike!

Like the nation of Israel, I need to stay continually watchful, prepared with the whole armor of God if I want to combat the temptations of the world, the flesh, and the devil. I have an enemy whose strategy is a sneak attack, especially when I'm weak. And I know that with all of the changes and upheavals in my life, I could become easy prey. From now on I need to wear the belt of truth at all times, along with the helmet of salvation, especially during wilderness times. And "In addition to all this, take up the shield of faith, with which you can extinguish all the flaming arrows of the evil one" (Ephesians 6:16).

> [God] brought his people out like a flock; he led them like sheep through the desert. He guided them safely, so they were unafraid. . . . Thus he brought them to the border of his holy land."
>
> Psalm 78:52–54

A New Prayer for the Journey

Heavenly Father,
Source of all life, I praise You for lovingly providing
us with everything we need. Just as You gave water

to the Israelites from a rock in the desert, You give us Jesus, the Living Water, and the promise that we will never thirst again. Forgive me for grumbling about this desert where I've been traveling. I see now that You long to use it to show me my helplessness, my need for You, and to teach me to trust You. Let this wilderness time in my life accomplish that work, Lord. Thank You for the companions You've given me for this journey. Help me to stop wallowing in my own misery and pride and remember that we were created to walk with each other, pray with each other. Show me someone I can be a companion to in this place. And restore to me the joy of my salvation, so that I might become a spring of life to other weary travelers.

Amen

3

THE JUDEAN
WILDERNESS

Ah, Sovereign Lord, you have made the heavens and the earth
by your great power and outstretched arm. Nothing is too
hard for you.

Jeremiah 32:17

We have left the Wilderness of Zin and traveled
north to explore a slightly less desolate desert,
the Judean Wilderness. Our first stop is Masada,
King Herod's mountain fortress. The site looks unpromising
from a distance, blending in with the surrounding sepia-toned
hills, but I'm learning that looks can be deceiving.

To reach the fortress more than 1,200 feet above us, we
have two choices: a forty-five-minute hike up the winding
Snake Path beneath the broiling desert sun, or a three-minute
ride in a modern cable car. I wave down at the people on the
Snake Path from my gondola. The view on my ascent leaves
me as breathless as the hikers must be. I can see for miles,

but aside from the aqua-blue Dead Sea in the distance, the savage terrain is the color of dry bones.

The Snake Path was the only way to the top when King Herod built Masada, yet I'm certain that he never hiked the steep slope to his desert hideaway. His plentiful slaves would have carried him up in a canopied sedan chair. King Herod was a man of great excesses, initiating dozens of huge, ambitious projects throughout Israel, including the entire city of Caesarea with its man-made harbor, the Tomb of the Patriarchs in Hebron, and a complete remodeling of the Temple complex in Jerusalem. But this fortress I'm about to visit in the middle of nowhere, on top of a nearly inaccessible mountain, is a monument to his paranoia. This is the same King Herod who slaughtered Bethlehem's babies in an attempt to kill his rival king, the infant Jesus. Herod also killed his wife and three of his own sons, along with countless enemies, real or imagined.

We soon reach the top and begin to explore the large plateau. It's nearly half a mile long and as wide as three football fields placed end-to-end. We walk through a maze of storehouses built to hold vast amounts of food supplies: wine, grain, and olive oil, along with weapons, of course. We descend a flight of some sixty stairs into an enormous underground cistern with thick plastered walls, capable of holding a million cubic feet of water. We all want to know where Herod found water in the middle of a bone-dry desert! Our guide explains how his ingeniously engineered dams and conduits captured every scant drop of rainfall flowing down from the surrounding hills and stored it in two underground cisterns. Paranoia can make a man very resourceful.

As I continue to tour the many buildings on this flat mountaintop, I begin to see that Herod had no intention of barricading himself inside an austere fortress. Masada has watchtowers and a thick wall around the perimeter of the mountaintop, but it also has every comfort that a decadent king might desire: a Roman-style bathhouse with frescoed walls; two palaces complete with bathtubs and mosaic floors; and even a private swimming pool. I hike down a series of stairs and walkways for a tour of Herod's northern palace. It is constructed on three terraces that hang precipitously off the prow of this ship-shaped mountain, reminding me of the young couple in the movie *Titanic*. The beautifully decorated rooms are strategically placed to catch the evening breezes as Herod gazed out at the Dead Sea in the distance. The spectacular "I'm-king-of-the-world" view also enabled him to see his enemies approaching.

Herod never had to flee to Masada to escape from his enemies, but a small remnant of Jewish patriots did. They climbed Masada with their families to escape from the Roman armies after Jerusalem and the Temple were destroyed. The Romans had slaughtered large numbers of their fellow Jews and carried off the rest into slavery. But thanks to Herod's stockpiles of food and water, the refugees were able to hide on Masada for several years. They were safe here, secure. Who would bother with the last few Jewish stragglers in the middle of a remote desert?

The Romans would. They were as fanatical about stamping out every last enemy as Herod had been, and they sent the Tenth Legion to besiege Masada. As I look down from the top, I can still see the neatly squared-off Roman encampments far below where the soldiers bivouacked. My stomach does a little turn, wondering how the Jewish families felt as they also looked down, knowing they were surrounded by well-armed, well-trained soldiers. The relentless enemy left them no escape, no option except surrender—and every man on Masada knew what the Romans would do to their wives and children if they did. We walk around to the western side of the fortress to see the man-made siege ramp that the Romans constructed to enable their soldiers to storm the fortress without using the Snake Path. They used captured Jewish slaves to build the ramp, knowing that Masada's defenders wouldn't attack their own people. I imagine the refugees' despair growing day after day along with the ramp.

We sit down in the ruins of Masada's synagogue to hear the rest of the story. When the ramp was completed and the Roman invasion was imminent, the remaining 960 Jewish refugees gathered here in the synagogue on the final night and made a suicide pact, choosing to die rather than watch their families be abused and enslaved by the Romans. The archaeologists who excavated Masada found a pile of potsherds with names on them—the lots that had been used to decide who would kill the women and children and then themselves. But they did one more thing as they huddled together in the synagogue to pray on that last night. Believing themselves to be the last surviving Jews in Israel, the defenders hid the scroll of the prophet Ezekiel beneath the floor—where archaeologists later found it—leaving it open to the thirty-seventh chapter. God had shown Ezekiel a valley of very dry human bones and asked, "Son of man, can these bones live?" Impossible. But the prophet replied, "O Sovereign Lord, you alone know" (v. 3).

For the surviving remnant on Masada who faced the fury of the Romans, the end of the Jewish nation looked certain. Israel's cities had been turned to rubble, the people carried away into slavery. Nothing remained except dry bones that could never live again. But after God showed Ezekiel the valley of dry bones, He said, "O my people, I am going to open your graves and bring you up from them; I will bring you back to the land of Israel. . . . I will take the Israelites out of the nations where they have gone. I will gather them from all around and bring them back into their own land" (Ezekiel 37:12, 21). And here I stand on the ruins of Masada over two thousand years later, and against all odds, Israel is a thriving nation with a population of more than seven million people. The land promised to Abraham and his descendants is once again theirs. God always keeps His promises. Even in times of cataclysmic upheaval and change, God's love and faithfulness are unchanging.

Appearances can be deceiving. When the Romans finally stormed the fortress of Masada and saw that the Jews were all dead, they believed they had stamped out the nation of Israel for good. When King Herod slaughtered the babies of Bethlehem, he believed he had prevented Israel's true King from taking His rightful throne. But nothing can defeat God's plans. Nothing. No matter how bleak or uncertain our circumstances may look, our loving Father is in control. "No, in all these things we are more than conquerors through him who loved us" (Romans 8:37).

Whenever the enemy seems victorious and I gaze at a valley of dry bones, whenever I face the end of a particular ministry or a job or a role that I have filled, I want to remember Masada. We serve a promise-keeping God, a God of miracles. My vigorous attempts to save myself, like Herod's, will never succeed. But what is impossible for man is always possible with God. When it seems as though all is lost and God asks, "Can these bones live?" let my answer be, "Sovereign Lord, you know."

Thirst

I have finished exploring Masada, so it's time for a rest. The Dead Sea hovers in the distance, a serene shade of turquoise blue. The water looks inviting, but for anyone who is thirsty, it may as well be a mirage. The salty, mineral-filled water is poisonous. I have floated in the Dead Sea—it's impossible to sink—and I found it very relaxing. But when even the tiniest drop of water splashed onto my lips, it tasted bitter. Some of the minerals extracted from the sea are used to make tranquilizers, which may explain why, after a few minutes of floating, everyone is laughing.

I find a bench near the Park Service office on Masada and sit down to admire the view while I wait for the rest of my group. That's when I notice a small outdoor sink with a water faucet. Where in the world does the water come from now that Herod's cisterns have dried up? Masada is on top of a mountain in the middle of the wilderness. How can there be a sink with fresh water way up here? I also notice that the faucet leaks—one tiny, sluggish drop every few seconds.

I'm still pondering the out-of-place sink when an interesting thing happens. Three frail brown birds fly over to land on a bare patch of ground a few yards away from me. *Birds?* They look as out of place as the sink. How can birds survive in such a desolate, treeless place? This isn't my backyard at home with lush foliage and feeders and a birdbath. There aren't any trees for miles and miles in any direction. Talk about a barren existence!

I sit very still, watching. The birds eye me nervously, as if to see if I'm going to harm them. Then one of them flutters up to perch on the water faucet. The bird pokes its beak into the hole and captures that one precious drop of water, then flies away. A second bird and then the third do the same. I can't imagine such a stingy, drop-by-drop subsistence.

Thirst is one of those consistent themes in Scripture that I often overlook—until a trip to Israel and a few hours beneath the desert sun remind me why water is such an important metaphor in the Bible. One of Israel's first complaints after liberation from slavery in Egypt was thirst. God showed His love and His commitment to a relationship with His people by providing an ample supply of water—from a rock! In the desert! Even after settling down in the Promised Land, the people remained aware of the preciousness of water and their need for God to provide rain. In a land without faucets, the Israelites had to return to their local wells and cisterns every day to replenish their supplies. "Give us this day our daily . . ." water.

My grandmother used to say, "You never miss the water till the well runs dry," but rarely in my suburban existence have I lacked water. I live near a seemingly endless supply of it in Lake Michigan. I can take a leisurely shower and run

Cistern

the sprinkler to water my parched lawn. Water flows, filtered and chilled, from my refrigerator door whenever I want it. Yet my monthly water bill is half the cost of my cell phone bill and Internet fees—modern life's necessities. Maybe we should use a new metaphor with the younger generation to get their attention, explaining that a life without God leaves us as helpless and disconnected as a life without Internet or cell phone service.

Thirst is a symptom of need, the body's way of telling me to take action. If I don't listen, I end up dehydrated and all sorts of bad things can happen, including loss of consciousness and death. Spiritual dryness is also a symptom: Something is wrong! Take action! I'm drying up! I need God. My soul's longing for God is as never-ending as my physical need for water. And spiritual dehydration leads to spiritual death. David recognized the parallels when he wrote, "As the deer pants for streams of water, so my soul pants for you, O God. My soul thirsts for God, for the living God" (Psalm 42:1–2). David isn't thirsting for a glitzy ritual at the Temple or an inspiring weekend retreat, but for a deep, abiding relationship with his Father.

Why do I often ignore my spiritual thirst, forgetting my soul's most basic requirement? Instead, when my weekly church services seem dry and my daily devotions don't satisfy, I blame it on the style of worship music or the new Bible translation I'm using. But the truth is, I can't sip from an hour-long church service on Sunday morning or dash off a hasty prayer or gulp down a daily Bible verse and expect them to sustain me any more than I can expect a glass of water to last for a week.

Jesus said, "Blessed are those who hunger and thirst for righteousness, for they will be filled" (Matthew 5:6). Living in a country like the United States, with an ample water supply, we miss the impact of His example. "Hunger and thirst" imply a desperation I've rarely experienced—until hiking here in the wilderness, that is. Back home, I fail to see the vastness of my need for righteousness, stretching in all directions like this desert. Nor do I always recognize the futility of trying to quench my thirst from our culture's reservoirs. Like the Dead Sea, they promise giddy pleasure and tranquility but the truth is, their waters will poison me if I drink from them. "My people have committed two sins," God told His people in Jeremiah's day. "They have forsaken me, the spring of living water, and have dug their own cisterns . . . that cannot hold water" (Jeremiah 2:13).

I don't need the world's cisterns. Just as God provided water in the wilderness to quench His people's thirst, He will quench my spiritual dehydration if I pay attention to my symptoms and recognize my need. Jesus said, "He who believes in me will never be thirsty" (John 6:35). Like the birds on Masada who have learned where the faucet is, I can go to the true Source.

Ah, but that would require spending *time* with God—more than an hour or two on Sunday, I suspect—getting to know Him, communing with Him, praising Him. And time, not water, is one of our culture's most precious commodities. And so I dash around in my busy life, giving God stingy drops of my time, checking Him off my to-do list, failing to pause and drink fully and deeply from my relationship with Him in prayer. No wonder my soul feels parched and dry.

In a land of plentiful water, I think we also forget the preciousness of the well of salvation, the high cost that Jesus paid to cleanse us from sin and clothe us in righteousness.

Would we squander His grace if we did, living unrighteous lives, allowing a shallow "sorry" to replace true repentance? It's no accident that one of the Old Testament's requirements for renewed purity for sinners was to wash their clothes and immerse themselves in a ritual bath, spending a resource as precious to them as gold—water. And Jesus ordained that our own symbolic cleansing should be through baptism in water. The good news is that His grace doesn't drip in tiny drops like this faucet on Masada but overflows to all who acknowledge their thirst.

The birds come and go as I watch them take turns at the stingy waterspout. I have to resist the urge to open the spigot and create a lavish puddle of water where they can splash and drink freely. I don't do that, of course. But I know a lot of people back home—more precious to God than sparrows—who are dying of thirst and need the water of life. I can lead them to the Source so they will never thirst again.

Stones and Sheep

Today we're hiking up a narrow, rocky path in the area where Christ's temptation took place. Like all of the other wilderness places I've seen, the acres and acres of featureless desert have no fences or boundaries or landmarks. The terrain seems inhospitable to any form of life. Yet when I stop to take a drink of water and eat a granola bar, I see movement on a nearby hill, as if the rocks have sprung to life and are milling around. Am I hallucinating from the searing sun?

The migrating rocks turn out to be a flock of shaggy sheep with wool the same dirty beige color as the desert. I watch as the shepherd leads them closer and closer to where I'm sitting, and I'm surprised to see that he is a young boy, ten or twelve years old. How will this child ever find his way home again? Doesn't his mother worry about him? This is my own fear talking. I find it impossible to stop worrying about my own children so far from home, though they are adults. I am no less worried about them now than when they were riding their tricycles in front of our house.

I notice that these sheep aren't wandering aimlessly. The shepherd seems to know where he is taking them. But why is he dragging them through such worthless pastureland with nothing to feed on except rocks? The sheep do have their heads down, as if grazing on something, but when I look down at the ground around my feet, all I see are a few scattered tufts of coarse grass growing among the rocks and dirt. Are you kidding me? The shepherd has led them all the way out here for this? These scraggly weeds will nourish them?

I've always pictured David's sheep feeding in a lush green meadow near a cool, babbling brook while he sat beneath a tree strumming his harp. But this shepherd, leading his flock through inhospitable terrain, is the true picture Jesus painted for us when He said, "I am the good shepherd; I know my sheep and my sheep know me . . . and I lay down my life for the sheep" (John 10:14–15). The reality of life as His disciple, as one of "the sheep of his pasture" (Psalm 100:3), is a life of complete helplessness in a harsh environment, trusting the shepherd to lead us and feed us.

I admit that it's hard for me to follow the Good Shepherd when the terrain is dry and the path is steep and rough. It's even harder to watch my children follow Him on their own wilderness journeys, as all of them have this past year. Why would He take them through the valley of the shadow of death?

Maybe it's because the Good Shepherd, like this shepherd boy, knows where to find food for His sheep. "Which of you," Jesus asks, "if his son asks for bread, will give him a stone?" (Matthew 7:9). A loving parent doesn't pass out rocks at the dinner table, yet sometimes the portion God hands us looks an awful lot like a stone—hard and unnourishing. Or like these sparse, unappetizing weeds. We have to trust that it isn't. We may have to search carefully and endure a long, hot desert walk, but the food that the Shepherd leads us to and the lessons we learn on our rugged walk will nourish and strengthen us for the road ahead.

Even the Good Shepherd himself "was led by the Spirit into the desert to be tempted." When Jesus grew hungry, Satan mocked Him saying, "If you are the Son of God, tell these stones to become bread" (Matthew 4:1, 3). In other words, take the easy way out, think of your own needs, find greener pastures than where God is leading you. It's so easy for us to believe that lie, to trust our eyes and not God, to forget that the long, hard way of the cross is the way to eternal life.

As the boy and his sorry-looking sheep move on to the next hill, I notice that there are a lot of places where the sheep could wander and become lost among the rocks. I'm guessing the boy would be in trouble if he arrived home with one of his father's sheep missing. In an open area without boundaries or fences, how does the shepherd manage to keep his flock together? That's one of the things I worry about the most, living as we do in a culture that no longer recognizes moral or ethical barriers. What will prevent my children from wandering off and becoming lost? Jesus answers my fear by explaining what the Good Shepherd promises to do: "Does he not leave the ninety-nine . . . and go after the lost sheep until he finds it?" (Luke 15:4).

On the night of the Last Supper, as Jesus was about to return to His Father, He gave an account of His little flock. "While I was with them, I protected them and kept them safe. . . . None has been lost except the one doomed to destruction so that Scripture would be fulfilled" (John 17:12). Jesus also promised that all of His sheep, including my children, would return safely home to the fold: "My sheep listen to my voice; I know them, and they follow me. I give them eternal life, and they shall never perish; no one can snatch them out of my hand. My Father, who has given them to me, is greater than all; no one can snatch them out of my Father's hand" (John 10:27–29).

Even though my children will struggle through changes and desert times in their lives, the Good Shepherd will make sure they find nourishment there. And if they do wander away, getting lost in a culture without boundaries, Jesus has promised to search for them and lead them back to the Father's fold where they will be safe for eternity. "Then he calls his friends and neighbors together and says, 'Rejoice with me; I have found my lost sheep'" (Luke 15:6). No terrain is too bleak, no distance too far that it will stop God from rescuing His own. I can cling to that promise. I can trust the Good Shepherd.

Engedi

Our last stop in the Judean Wilderness is the Engedi Nature Reserve near the Dead Sea, a dozen miles north of Masada. According to the Bible, this is where David hid from King

Saul "near the Crags of the Wild Goats" (1 Samuel 24:2). Our group files out of the bus and starts climbing a steep, narrow trail. We are definitely in David's hiding place because there are both crags and mountain goats here. Long-horned ibex amble across the rocky slopes as if they have suction cups attached to their hooves, taunting gravity. Furry brown *coneys*, which remind me of prairie dogs, scamper between the stones, poking up their heads now and then to stare back at us.

The trail is arduous. We ascend a slender cleft between car-sized boulders. Why in the world would God tell David to hide here? The lifeless Dead Sea blocks his escape to the east, and nothing but barren wilderness stretches in the other three directions. Where would David find water for himself and his four hundred men? How would they survive the scorching sun in a land without trees—or sunblock? If these men were "in distress and discontented" when they joined up with David, I don't see their mood improving out here.

Gradually, we begin to see more and more green plants sprouting between the stones. Then I hear it—the sound of rushing, splashing, cascading water. We've arrived at an oasis. The air feels cool and refreshing after the difficult climb. The cold, spring-fed water is good to drink, the foliage lush and beautiful. This could be a lagoon in a Florida resort. Other tourists, including a group of young people with towels and bathing suits, are swimming and frolicking in the large, clear pool beneath the waterfall. Finding Eden in the middle of a dry, barren wilderness is so unexpected that I can imagine David's surprise and relief when he and his men arrived here, hot and weary and thirsty. I see them stripping off their sweaty tunics to splash in the refreshing water, giddy with laughter. Clearly God was looking out for them after all.

Discovering an oasis in the wilderness shouldn't surprise me. Again and again in Scripture and in life, I have seen God faithfully provide a time and place of refreshment for His weary children. It might be as unlikely as this freshwater pool near the Dead Sea or a weekend spiritual retreat at my church. Typically, I have to expend effort to get there. Finding time in my busy schedule or money on a tight budget requires as much effort as scaling a rocky mountain slope. It also requires me to be honest about my barren spiritual condition and willing to admit I'm in need of relief. It's easier to camp beside the Dead Sea's bitter waters mumbling, "Poor me. Why doesn't God help me? Why can't I feel His presence?" than it is to search and climb and stretch spiritual muscles that have become flabby from lack of use.

Wallowing in self-pity is hypnotic, as mesmerizing as floating in the Dead Sea. Unlike a body of freshwater, where I have to paddle to stay afloat, the Dead Sea's dense waters allow me to drift on my back for hours and hours, expending little energy. This lethargy is habit-forming. The bitter, poisonous waters of self-pity are the wrong place to come to quench a dry soul. And if you float in the Dead Sea or in self-pity long enough and drift far enough, you'll end up in enemy territory on the opposite shore—in this case, the land of Israel's ancient enemy the Moabites.

The rugged mountains of Moab on the other side of the Dead Sea—now in the nation of Jordan—are clearly visible from our Engedi oasis. I find it interesting that the nation of Moab was birthed from self-pity. During the cataclysm that turned this once-fertile plain into the barren place that it is today—the destruction of Sodom and Gomorrah—two sisters were jolted from sleep in the middle of the night and told to run for their lives. Imagine their panic as they fled Sodom with the earth quaking beneath their feet and the night sky eerily illuminated with fire. Chunks of brimstone rained down around them, and screams of terror and pain echoed behind them as they staggered forward, inhaling the stench of sulfur and death. Their father, Lot, urged them toward the safety of the mountains, shouting, "Run! Don't look back!" But their mother did look back, and suddenly she was no longer running alongside them. The terrified sisters didn't dare to turn around to see what had become of her.

The night seemed endlessly long, the climb steep, but when dawn finally arrived, the sisters gazed down with their father at their ruined world. Shaken and stunned, they saw nothing but smoke and destruction. The catastrophe reduced their home, their city, to smoldering ashes. Everyone was dead. The girls' faces reflected the same dull, stunned horror that we see in the survivors of earthquakes and tornadoes and hurricanes.

Days passed in despair and sorrow, until self-pity began to whisper to the sisters that God had abandoned them. They believed self-pity's lie and decided that if they were going to survive, they needed to come up with a plan. "Our father is old," one sister reasoned, "and there is no man around here to lie with us, as is the custom all over the earth. Let's get our father to drink wine and then lie with him" (Genesis 19:31–32). Self-pity spawned sin, and both sisters gave birth to sons from their incestuous relationship. One named her child Moab, meaning "from father," and it's from him that the nation of Moab originated.

I'm grateful for this pilgrimage, a wiser choice than staying home and wallowing in self-pity. While I don't have to leave home to find God's oasis, I do have to search for it, pursuing

God in prayer and trusting Him to take care of me when all other hope is gone. He promised that "If . . . you seek the Lord your God, you will find him if you look for him with all your heart and with all your soul" (Deuteronomy 4:29). Like David and his men, I have to turn my back on the lifeless Dead Sea and start climbing.

Now that we've arrived in this cool glade, our guide has us sit down in the shade of an overhanging rock. He explains that this was once a cave that collapsed during an earthquake or a flash flood. It might even be the cave where David and his men hid from King Saul. Saul's pursuit of David also began with a bout of self-pity after he heard the maidens of Israel hailing his victorious army with their song: "Saul has slain his thousands, and David his tens of thousands" (1 Samuel 18:7). Self-pity gave birth to murderous jealousy, and Saul decided that David was his enemy and had to die.

As I sit in this remnant of a cave, I wonder why David hid instead of fighting back. He was a seasoned warrior; the men with him were desperate enough to fight when cornered. Saul's forces outnumbered theirs by seven to one, but unlikely odds hadn't stopped David in the past. As a boy, he had challenged a giant more than twice his size while other warriors cowered in fear. Wouldn't logic tell David to fight, winning the promised kingdom through a military victory the way countless other leaders had come to power? Instead, David hid in a cave and waited for God to give him the throne. To a celebrated warrior, running and hiding must have felt cowardly. Waiting is always harder than doing something.

David had a lot of time to talk with God while hiding here. The Engedi oasis is peaceful, with water gurgling and birds twittering and leaves rustling in the wind. He composed some of his most poignant psalms, revealing his struggles to trust in God, psalms that still offer strength and hope today in times of change. Reading Psalm 57, written during this time in David's life, I can hear his impatience—and maybe just a twinge of self-pity. Won't this pursuit ever end? I'm tired of it! Tired of living in a damp, sunless cave. I'm supposed to be the king. David poured out his sorrow, but even when tempted to feel sorry for himself, he always ended his psalms with hope and trust. "For great is your love, reaching to the heavens; your faithfulness reaches to the skies" (v. 10). David managed to take his eyes off his bleak situation and look up to God, trusting His timing.

These are lessons I want to grasp, yet the only way to learn them is to be deprived of my own resources: to hunger and thirst, to be uncomfortable, to feel pursued and unjustly wronged. It might even mean suffering through a catastrophic change, like Lot's daughters did, and questioning why God would allow this to happen. It might mean waiting for God's promises, wrestling with unanswered prayer. And waiting some more.

One day, high in his oasis hideaway, David was given an opportunity to change his miserable situation. King Saul left his army at the base of the trail and climbed up to the cave alone to relieve himself. "This is a God-given opportunity!" David's men must have whispered to him from their hiding place in the shadows. "You can kill Saul and end our misery and exile!" Was God finally answering his prayers?

David crept toward his enemy, but instead of killing Saul, he cut off the corner of his garment, then scurried back into the darkness. The Torah required all Jewish men to sew blue tassels on the corners of their garments as daily reminders of God's commandments. One of those commandments was "Thou shall not kill," yet Saul was seeking to kill David without a just cause, using his kingly power and Israel's army to do it. By cutting off Saul's fringes, David sent Saul a clear message: You're breaking God's commandments. And perhaps the tassels reminded David of his obligation to obey God, as well. David could have killed Saul but he didn't. He refused to succumb to self-pity and take matters into his own hands as Lot's daughters had. God would put David on the throne when the time was right. David didn't see Saul's vulnerability as an answer to prayer but as a temptation to sin.

Imagine the angry whispering and wrestling in the back of that cave when David returned with a handful of tassels instead of Saul's head. It must have taken quite a struggle for David to restrain his men from doing what he had refused to do. David had sworn an oath of allegiance to Saul before God, and he refused to break that oath or murder a defenseless man. When we truly trust God, we're able to extend His grace, even to people like Saul who don't deserve it. Vengeance belongs to God.

After King Saul returned to his waiting army, David strode to the mouth of the cave and stood where Saul and his men could see him. He might have been within range of their sharpshooters' arrows, but David wasn't afraid. If God's promises were true and he was destined to be king, then he need "not fear . . . the arrow that flies by day" (Psalm 91:5). David shouted down to Saul, "I cut off the corner of your robe but did not kill you. Now understand and recognize that I am not guilty of wrongdoing or rebellion" (1 Samuel 24:11). David took a huge risk. He and his men would be trapped in the cave with no way out if Saul ordered his superior forces to climb up and fight. Instead, Saul recognized that David, his supposed enemy, had shown him mercy. Saul stopped chasing him and went home.

David did not go home. Nothing changed for him. He remained in the wilderness with a pack of disgruntled misfits as he continued to wait to be crowned king. And as he had feared, Saul later relapsed into paranoia and started pursuing him all over again.

How did David know to wait and not fight? I'm a planner, a worrier. I need to figure everything out and take action, not sit still. But time and again God has tumbled this Scripture verse from Isaiah into my path like a car-sized boulder: "They that wait upon the Lord shall renew their strength; they shall mount up with wings as eagles; they shall run, and not be weary; and they shall walk, and not faint" (40:31 KJV). The first time I encountered this promise from God was more than thirty years ago as I struggled to get pregnant. I already had one child and desperately longed for a second, but after four years of waiting, my prayers continued to go unanswered. I drifted so far into the waters of self-pity that I could no longer walk down the diaper aisle in the grocery store or share my friends' joy when they became pregnant.

Then came what I thought was a God-given opportunity to adopt a baby. I learned of an unmarried girl with an unplanned pregnancy who was about to have an abortion. Without taking time to pray or seek God's wisdom, I sprang into action, halting the abortion with promises to pay all of the young woman's medical expenses and adopt her child. But all of my hopes and plans—the decorated nursery, the new crib, the drawers full of sweet baby clothes—had to be abandoned when she decided to keep her baby. I could have saved myself endless heartache if I had consulted God first instead of taking matters into my own hands.

God continued to speak His promise to me: "They that wait upon the Lord shall renew their strength." And I did wait—a total of seven and a half years, feeling much like David as he waited in this cave. But in God's perfect timing, David did become Israel's king. And when my time of waiting came to an end, God blessed me with not one more child, but with two.

Isaiah says of Christ: "He will not judge by what he sees with his eyes, or decide by what he hears with his ears" (11:3). As we surrender control of our lives and become more like Christ, we'll also grow in discernment—and in patience. David had these qualities; Lot's daughters didn't. I need them. I can't follow my own instincts and emotions or use human reasoning to know which opportunities are from God and which are not. My eyes often deceive me. From down below, standing on the shore of the Dead Sea, I never would have guessed there was an oasis like this one in the barren wilderness.

When we take the time to seek God's wisdom for our dilemmas, He enables us to see things His way and wait for His perfect timing. Through the eyes of faith, we'll see that Goliath can be slain—and that Saul shouldn't be harmed. Lot's daughters, living in the corrosive atmosphere of Sodom, had lost their ability to see.

David did the right thing—and did God instantly reward him? No. He continued to live in the wilderness. He continued to wait—as I continue to wait for many of my prayers to be answered. But like David, I know that "they that wait upon the Lord shall renew their strength . . . they shall run, and not be weary."

As I leave the Engedi oasis, following the trail downhill to the bus, the distant mountains of Moab glow in the desert sun, tinted the soft pink color of seashells. I take time to pray as I descend, asking God to help me be content where I am, with the provisions and the companions He has given me. Content to wait for the promises yet to come, even if I seem to be waiting in a barren place.

We have heard with our ears, O God; our fathers have told us what you did in their days, in days long ago. . . . It was not by their sword that they won the land, nor did their arm bring them victory; it was your right hand, your arm, and the light of your face, for you loved them.

Psalm 44:1, 3

A New Prayer for the Journey

Sovereign Lord,
Nothing is impossible for You. You are a promise-keeping God, able to do so much more for Your children than we could ever ask or imagine. I confess that I have ignored the symptoms of my spiritual thirst for too long and failed to acknowledge my need for You. Forgive me for indulging in self-pity as I have waited, and for turning to my own solutions instead of trusting Your perfect timing. Please use this time of change in my life to teach me Your faithfulness and Your love. Thank You for your promise to rescue me and my loved ones whenever we wander away from You like lost sheep. Breathe life into my dry bones, Lord, so that I may truly live again.
Amen

4

CROSSING THE JORDAN

Now then, you and all these people, get ready to cross the Jordan River into the land I am about to give to them . . . Be strong and very courageous. Be careful to obey all the law my servant Moses gave you; do not turn from it to the right or to the left, that you may be successful wherever you go.

Joshua 1: 2, 7

The Jordan River is not impressive. Like most tourists who envision a river of Mississippi proportions, I was disappointed when I saw it for the first time. From where I'm looking at it now, near a popular baptismal spot, an average swimmer could paddle across the sluggish green water and back again without much trouble. I'm guessing that the river was much wider and more imposing in biblical times, before modern Israelis began tapping into it for drinking water and irrigation.

But the Jordan River doesn't need to be impressive in order to fulfill its role as a dividing line, a place of demarcation between old and new. Just as crossing the Red Sea represented freedom from the past for Israel and a way out of slavery in Egypt, crossing the Jordan meant the end of their desert wanderings and the beginning of their new life in the Promised Land. For Christians, our life-changing boundary is our baptism into a new life with Christ. We're no longer condemned to wander through life, aimless and thirsty, or to live enslaved to the taskmaster of sin. It was no coincidence that Jesus' baptism took place here in the Jordan River.

As Moses and the Israelites camped on the Jordan River's opposite shore, excitement must have prickled through the community like electricity. Their dreary desert journey had come to an end; they were crossing over into a new life. But Moses was about to die, and before he did, he stood before the people to deliver a final, pleading sermon. He recalled Israel's experience of salvation and provision in the wilderness and enumerated God's promised blessings in the future if the people obeyed Him. Moses concluded with these impassioned words: "See, I set before you today life and prosperity, death and destruction. . . . Now choose life, so that you and your children may live and that you may love the Lord your God, listen to his voice, and hold fast to him. For the Lord is your life" (Deuteronomy 30:15, 19–20). It was the same choice that God gave Adam and Eve in the Garden of Eden: They could choose to obey God and live, or choose the forbidden tree and die.

We make the same choice when we decide to follow Christ, leaving behind disobedience and death and entering into new life. "Therefore, if anyone is in Christ, he is a new creation; the old has gone, the new has come!" (2 Corinthians 5:17).

"I have come that they may have life," Jesus said, "and have it to the full" (John 10:10). And so we choose life and cross over through baptism to plant our feet firmly in the kingdom of God. Here we can build new lives, grow and prosper if we continue to listen to His voice and hold fast to Him. Except for one *slight* detail . . . this new land is currently occupied by our enemies. Deeply entrenched enemies.

As soon as Joshua led the Israelites across the Jordan, they, too, faced enemies: giant enemies nine feet tall; enemies living in fortified cities with high, thick walls; armed enemies who were unwilling to give up an inch of territory. Many of us naïvely believed that once we became Christians and entered God's Promised Land, our lives would immediately become heavenly. We could stake out our little plot of land, sow some seeds, and before long we'd be harvesting fruit for the kingdom. But wait . . . not so fast. We might have entered the kingdom of God, but we still have territory to conquer, temptations to face, and a host of old, familiar enemies who need to be put to death.

My old habits die hard, especially the bad ones. Old patterns of thinking and behaving can be as difficult to conquer as the Canaanite fortress of Jericho. Paul talks about this warfare in Romans 8, and delivers the same type of impassioned sermon that Moses did. "If you live according to the sinful nature, you will die; but if by the Spirit you put to death the misdeeds of the body, you will live" (v. 13). I can almost hear Paul shouting, like Moses, "Choose life!"

Sometimes it seems easier to negotiate a peace treaty and allow our old nature to live peaceably beside our new nature in Christ than to do battle with our flesh. "I've always had a bad temper," we say, making excuses. Or, "The people in my family always gossip . . . or tell little white lies . . . or hold grudges. It's in my genes." But doesn't that verse in Romans 8 say *put to death* the misdeeds of the body? That sounds like warfare, to me. It sounds like the same instructions God gave concerning the enemies in the Promised Land: leave no inhabitants. "If you do not drive out the inhabitants of the land," Moses warned, "those you allow to remain will become barbs in your eyes and thorns in your sides" (Numbers 33:55). I've felt those barbs and thorns lately, and I know that it's time to conquer some enemies.

I'm standing at a new Jordan River in my walk with God, on the shores of new changes in my life. I've been wandering through a dry, monotonous desert back home in need of His direction. But just as I've had my fill of hiking in Israel's wilderness these past few days, I'm also ready to leave my old life behind and cross over. I have old habits, entrenched ways of thinking, and numerous other strongholds in my life that I need to conquer. One of those battles will be to replace my image of what I wanted my future to be like with God's vision for me. I don't know why I've been so reluctant to tear down those false images. The Bible promises that "No eye has seen, no ear has heard, no mind has conceived what God has prepared for those who love him" (1 Corinthians 2:9).

I want to be like Caleb, one of only two faithful spies who saw God's vision for the Promised Land instead of what the ten other spies saw. The others saw giants and walled cities and inhabitants who made them feel like mere grasshoppers. Caleb saw a land flowing with milk and honey and enemies who didn't stand a chance against the God who had delivered him from slavery in Egypt. When the ten faithless spies had died off and Caleb finally got to choose his promised inheritance forty years later, he said this: "So here I am today, eighty-five years old! I am still as strong today as the day Moses sent me out; I'm just as vigorous to go out to battle now as I was then. Now give me this hill country that the Lord promised me that day. You yourself heard then that the Anakites were there and their cities were large and fortified, but, the Lord helping me, I will drive them out just as he said" (Joshua 14:10–12). Caleb didn't sit back and watch the younger men fight. He refused to pick an easily-won patch of land for his inheritance. Courageous? Certainly. But the knowledge that he wasn't fighting alone fueled his courage. As he told his fellow Israelites, God is fighting for us and with us.

The Jordan River may seem puny and disappointing to other pilgrims, but I'm inspired by it. I see myself standing before a vast new territory waiting to be conquered, beginning with my own sinful habits and false images. A territory where I can plant seeds of faith and watch them bear fruit. Jesus has a kingdom that I can help build when I get home, and I don't want to sit back in any area of my life and let younger, more energetic Christians do all the work—and have all the fun. As I cross a new Jordan, I want to say, like Caleb, "Give me the mountain with the giants!"

At the Crossroads

I love maps. Whenever I travel, I keep a map on hand so I can orient myself to the bigger picture of where I am and where I'm going. I've decided to travel through Israel with two maps. One is of the modern nation with its neighbors and highways, cities and landmarks. The second is a map of the region in ancient times, showing enemy nations such as Moab, Edom, and the Philistines. Studying these two maps is very sobering. Israel seems so small compared to the rest of the world, a tiny guppy swimming among sharks. How will she survive?

The patch of land that God gave to Abraham and his descendants perches on the crossroads of the ancient empires of history. To get from Pharaoh's domain in Egypt to the kingdoms of Babylon or Assyria, you have to travel right through Israel. When Alexander the Great of Greece or the conquering Roman emperors decided to expand toward Persia and the golden empires of the east, Israel lay right along their path. The broad, flat plains of the Jordan River where I'm now traveling provide an easily accessible highway for marching armies, then and now.

If God wanted to pick a place where His chosen people could live and prosper and form a nation governed by His laws, why didn't He put them on an island, like Fiji, in the middle of the Pacific? Why not select a more isolated piece of land protected by steep mountains or formidable deserts? Why put the people He loved on the intersection of a busy street between powerful pagan empires? For that matter, why hasn't God told Christians to retreat to small, isolated communities, far away from everything that's wrong with our culture, and live like the Amish?

Maybe it's because spiritual growth and vibrant faith in God don't happen in isolation, but under pressure. Without the danger of threats from Pharaoh, we never would have to decide if we're going to trust in our own chariots and horses, or in God. Maybe we can see more clearly what we believe and who we are when we're able to contrast our faith to other nations who don't know God, holding them side by side like before-and-after pictures. Our faith often grows stronger when we have to defend our beliefs, the same way that patriotism flowers and blooms when our country is threatened. And for most of us, our prayer life certainly flourishes when we're under siege; they say there are no atheists in foxholes.

Of course, with so much exposure to other cultures, the temptation to abandon God and adopt the ways of the surrounding, invading nations becomes a powerful lure. This temptation is especially strong for the second and third generations who haven't experienced God's presence and miracles firsthand, only by word of mouth. And once we settle down and build homes and plant vineyards, we tend to get complacent. That's what happened in Israel again and again. And it's what I'm continually tempted to do.

I want the American Dream of a home in the suburbs, an SUV in the garage, and all of the other toys and trinkets of modern American life, just like my neighbors have. I want to reinforce my future security with retirement investments and insurance plans—the fortresses and arsenals of modern life. I want to look respectable and be accepted by my neighbors as badly as the Israelites did when they asked God to give them a king like the other nations. Israel got Saul for their king and rejected God. I do the same thing whenever building the American Dream becomes more important to me than building God's kingdom. And whenever my resources, time, and passion go into living the good life instead of the godly life.

The other danger for Israel, living at the crossroads, came during times when foreign oppressors tried to systematically stamp out their religion. One of those oppressors was the ruthless monarch Antiochus Epiphanes, who made it illegal for the Jews to study the Torah or practice their faith. He slaughtered thousands of faithful Jews who refused to obey him, and he culminated his apostasy by sacrificing a pig on God's altar in the Temple in Jerusalem. His tyranny led to the rise of a group called the Pharisees—the separate ones—who were fanatically committed to fighting for and clinging to God's Law. A second group, the Maccabees, took up arms as freedom fighters and managed to win back the nation and their Temple. Jews still celebrate their victory and the miracle of the menorah lights at Hanukkah.

It might be easier to combat an invading culture when it comes in the form of a tyrannical ruler and clearly drawn battle lines. But more often the invasions in our lives are subtle. When my children were young, I waged a constant struggle to separate Christianity from culture. How, for example, could we celebrate Jesus' birth in a meaningful way when the secular culture had hijacked our holy day and turned it into a spending extravaganza with Santa Claus? How could we make the joy of Christ's resurrection clear when that day had become an Easter egg hunt? It's not always easy to separate God's truth from cultural tradition and teach our children and grandchildren what faith is all about.

Lately, the battle between Christianity and popular culture seems to be heating up. The standards of Christian morality used to be accepted as the norm in America, even if they weren't necessarily practiced. Today, our culture calls me intolerant if I don't condone its standards of morality, and it tries to coerce me into agreement. It's at this time when I again ask why God didn't put Christians on an island, where we could quietly live a life of community and love according to Christ's teachings.

But as much as I may wish for isolation, it was never God's plan for Israel or for us. The book of Acts pictures the early church as a vibrant, growing community in Jerusalem until persecution and exile scattered believers throughout the Roman Empire. Exile forced believers to follow Christ while living smack-dab in the middle of pagan Roman society. God gave Abraham this piece of land on the crossroads of the nations because He had promised that the world would be blessed through Abraham's descendants. Jesus came to be a light to the Gentiles, and His light needs to shine through us, His body. We have to stand at the world's crossroads if we want the world to see that light.

God also puts His people in the middle of things for the same reason that He put the tree of temptation in the middle of the Garden—so that our choice to follow Him would be a conscious, daily one. Every time we publicly choose to live for Christ, He is glorified. It's simpler, no doubt, to live an obedient life on an island than on Wall Street—but what a statement a Christian lifestyle could make there. All of Israel's neighboring nations were amazed at a people who worshiped one God in a temple that contained no images. A life lived by the morality of the Torah produced a vivid contrast to the idolatrous, immoral, perverted ways of the surrounding nations. The Torah even prescribed the clothing that the Jews were to wear and the food they could and could not eat. They were told how to cut their hair and trim their beards and were commanded to rest from their work on the Sabbath. Following all of these laws was to be a conscious choice, done out of love for God and in obedience to His Word, whether it made any sense to a watching world or not. Did wearing tassels on their garments and refusing to eat pork really make some magical, mysterious difference? God seemed to think so.

We are "Exhibit A" to a world that's indifferent to God. How else will they see the difference between a life lived with

God and one lived without Him except by our example? If I'm lying in a hospital ward beside an atheist, I hope she'll see a clear contrast between the way I face pain and death and the way she does. She should also need sunglasses as the body of Christ shines His glory throughout the room, gathering around me to offer prayer and support.

The interesting thing is that the faith God handed down to Moses has endured in spite of their location on the crossroads. No other religious system—Roman, Assyrian, Babylonian, Egyptian, or Canaanite—is still being followed and practiced by its descendants four thousand years later despite such outrageous obstacles as enemy invasions, exile, and dispersion. All around me in this land, I see telltale tassels dangling from men's garments; flourishing Kosher restaurants and butcher shops; Torah study centers and day schools spilling over with students. And every Sabbath, the stores in Jerusalem close their doors, the public buses and trains stop running, and the Jewish people cease their labor for a day of rest. This nation, this enduring Jewish faith, are testimonies to the world of God's faithfulness and love.

What about us? Our Christian faith is still being practiced two thousand years after Jesus' resurrection. The kingdom is still growing, His Word is still being taught. It might be harder to take a stand as a Christian these days, but maybe that's a good thing. The practice of my faith can't be—shouldn't be—rote or routine the way I've allowed it to become. It needs to be a conscious, daily choice, not motivated by peer pressure or law the way that the Taliban or Iran's morality police enforce Islam. The central reason for choosing to follow Christ in my daily life should be my deep love for God. I was called, chosen, loved, and redeemed by Him, just as

Israel was. My response to such love and grace should be the natural one of love and obedience in return.

God promised Abraham that through him the whole world would be blessed. He fulfilled that promise in Abraham's descendant, Jesus Christ. As His followers, living at the crossroads of nations and cultures, we are also called to be a blessing to the world. Are we? God has graciously provided us with a road map—His holy Word. We all have friends and relatives and co-workers who are lost or heading in the wrong direction. What a blessing we would be to them if we stood at the crossroads and pointed to the right path.

Up to Jerusalem

For years I have blithely read in the Bible how Jesus and His disciples went *up* to Jerusalem, but today I'm experiencing the full impact of that simple, two-letter word—UP. What a hard climb it is from the plains of the Jordan River *up* to Jerusalem. The road ascends some 3,800 feet in only fourteen miles. Our tour bus labors up the slope, the driver shifting and downshifting, the engine whining and protesting. I can't imagine making this pilgrimage on foot, hiking up this steep road with my extended family, carrying piles of bedding and food and livestock for my offerings. But I can imagine the conversation that might have taken place because I've heard it on countless family car trips: "Are we there yet?" "I'm tired." "I'm thirsty." "Quit complaining!"

Going up to Jerusalem requires stamina. Three times a year, pilgrims from Galilee, including Jesus and His disciples, would have followed the Jordan River south to Jericho near

Mount Zion Today

the Dead Sea, then taken this road up—and up—to Jerusalem. The Dead Sea is the lowest place on earth at 1,300 feet below sea level, and Jerusalem is situated at 2,550 feet above sea level. It requires hard work and sacrifice to worship God. It's much easier to stay home and forget the long journey, but according to Jewish law, the people were required to go three times a year for the three annual festivals as soon as they were old enough to walk. Moses had warned the Israelites that they were in danger of forgetting their history and their God once they settled down in homes and villages. And whenever Israel backslid into idolatry, they stopped making these pilgrimages. The national revivals begun by good kings such as Hezekiah and Josiah always began by renewing the celebration of Passover and the other feasts.

In each of the three pilgrimage festivals, the Israelites reenacted a portion of their history so they would never forget it. At Passover they relived the night in Egypt when they daubed blood on their doorposts so that the angel of death would pass over their homes. For Pentecost, they reenacted the day that God gave the Torah on Mount Sinai and they responded, "Whatever the Lord says, we will do" (see Deuteronomy 5:27). During the Feast of Tabernacles, they ate and slept in flimsy huts, open to the skies, to recall their desert wanderings. The three pilgrimages also reminded them of their ancestor Abraham who journeyed with God beneath the open skies his entire life. That long walk demonstrated that our spiritual life will always be a continuing journey of faith.

Our bus continues to climb up and up. Soon we reach a dividing line between the dry desert and the green highlands. The mountains around Jerusalem form a boundary line—green to the west, thanks to the moist Mediterranean air; dry and brown to the east, where that moisture never reaches. This forms a visual picture of a life with God and a life without Him. Without the water of God's Word, without Christ the living water, there is only death and desolation. As the pilgrims ascended on their journey, climbing up from death to life, they experienced a visual picture of what God's Word meant in their lives—and in our lives.

I'm told that the Temple roof, adorned with the equivalent of $3 billion dollars in gold, was visible from a distance, shining in the sunlight as pilgrims approached. Jerusalem itself is a golden city, constructed from the creamy golden limestone found in that region. I can understand the pilgrims' excitement and anticipation when they finally glimpsed the city and the Temple in the distance. After the long journey, after the hard climb, they would be able to relax and rest and celebrate the festivals with feasting and joy. In describing the feasts in the Torah, God says over and over, "Rejoice!" And in all of the feasts that I've celebrated with my Jewish friends, I've eaten until I was stuffed, laughed until my sides ached, and gone to bed with peace in my heart. It's the same joy and relief I experience on Easter morning after the somber soul-searching of Good Friday—death transformed into life.

The annual pilgrimages to Jerusalem remind us that our spiritual life is not only a journey but a cycle of journeys. We'll never fully arrive until we reach heaven. But while we're here on earth we can continue to move toward a higher goal, "so that the body of Christ may be built up until we all reach unity in the faith and in the knowledge of the Son of God and become mature, attaining to the whole measure of the fullness of Christ" (Ephesians 4:12–13). Up and up. It's important not to stay home like spiritual infants, resting on past glories and miracles, content with the relationship we had with Christ when we first became born again. It's important that we keep moving toward God, climbing and sacrificing and remembering.

Remembering is important. As Joshua led the Israelites into the Promised Land to conquer and settle it, he erected "stones of remembrance," a series of seven stone memorials so that the people could look back and say, "Yes, God is faithful. He brought me this far and gave me victory in this place." The first memorial was comprised of stones taken from the Jordan riverbed, one for each tribe, as they crossed the river on dry land (Joshua 4:1–7). The final memorial was erected in Shechem, when Joshua and the people renewed their covenant with God after the land had been conquered. "When your descendants ask their fathers, 'What do these stones mean?' tell them . . . [God] did this so that all the peoples of the earth might know that the hand of the Lord is powerful and so that you might always fear the Lord your God" (Joshua 4:21, 24).

I've fallen into a monotonous routine back home because I have wanted to stay in one place when I should have moved forward. I've forgotten that discipleship is a journey. Now as I determine to start walking up to Jerusalem, continuing my walk with God, I want to mark the places where He has been faithful with stones of remembrance, revisiting them, never forgetting them. "Count your blessings, name them one by one . . . See what God has done," the old gospel song reminds us. And after remembering, I want to move forward and celebrate what God is doing today, then ask Him what His plans are for tomorrow. How should I live during the next stage of my journey?

When I look at this rugged terrain and the steep, breathless climb to Jerusalem, I wonder why we have tried to make the Christian life a comfortable one. Why are we tempted to make our faith experiences all about "arriving," finding a great parking spot, resting on our achievements, building monuments and settling down? I was guilty of doing just that when I imagined that after raising three children for Christ they would settle down beside me and we'd all live happily ever after, serving Him within the static confines of our home church. Or when I became so comfortable with the ministry God has given me that I stopped looking for new ways to use my gifts and talents to serve Him. I'm learning that the spiritual life is all about change—moving forward and going steadily upward, growing closer and closer to God. It's about sacrificing my will and my plans to His.

I'm reminded of another old gospel song, "I have decided to follow Jesus . . . No turning back, no turning back." I often forget that the only way I can follow someone is if we are both moving, not sitting still. If we want to follow Jesus we must remain in motion, hiking behind Him as He walks forward in a chosen direction—up to Jerusalem.

The gospel of Mark says, "They were on their way up to Jerusalem, with Jesus leading the way, and . . . he took the Twelve aside and told them what was going to happen to him" (Mark 10:32). What He revealed was not at all what they had imagined. "'We are going up to Jerusalem,' he said, 'and the Son of Man will be betrayed to the chief priests and teachers of the law. They will condemn him to death and will hand him over to the Gentiles, who will mock him and spit on him, flog him and kill him. Three days later he will rise'" (Mark 10:33–34).

Jesus also said, "If anyone would come after me, he must deny himself and take up his cross and follow me. For whoever wants to save his life will lose it, but whoever loses his life for me will find it" (Matthew 16:24–25).

"Are we there yet? . . . I'm tired . . . I'm thirsty . . ."

No turning back. No turning back.

Good Samaritans

This road between Jerusalem and Jericho is where Jesus' parable of the Good Samaritan takes place. In the story, a traveler is ambushed and beaten by robbers and left for dead. The modern highway is a steep, winding road, bordered by cliffs and mountains and ravines; I can see how it would provide plenty of places for outlaws to hide and ambush unsuspecting travelers. This was a main road in Jesus' day, not only for pilgrims coming to attend the feasts but also for Jerusalem's wealthy citizens who loved to travel down to the spa and hot springs in Jericho. And the Temple priests were among the very wealthiest Israelites.

As I climb this road and see the setting of the parable, I open my Bible and read the entire account (Luke 10:25–37). The story is part of an extended conversation that Jesus had with an expert in the Law. This expert already knew all the right answers but he "stood up to test Jesus," posing the question, "What must I do to inherit eternal life?" Jesus answered with questions of His own: "What is written in the Law? How do you read it?" Rabbis and disciples always taught and learned this way, posing questions, searching for answers, digging into the tiniest details of what each word and letter in that word meant. In fact, Jewish schools still teach Torah this way.

The expert gave a very orthodox, acceptable reply to Jesus' question: "Love the Lord your God and love your neighbor," two commandments found in Deuteronomy 6:5 and Leviticus 19:18. "You have answered correctly," Jesus replied. "Do this and you will live." But the discussion wasn't over for this legal expert because "he wanted to justify himself, so he asked Jesus, 'And who is my neighbor?'" He wanted a checklist, a set of definite rules and regulations so he would know exactly who he was required to love and who he was not, when he was required to love them, and where, and how. Maybe then he could find a loophole that would excuse him. Jesus answered the question "Who is my neighbor?" with the parable of the Good Samaritan.

A Jewish traveler on this Jericho road was attacked and left for dead. The first person to pass by was a priest who didn't stop to help him. In fact, the priest made a wide circuit around the man. The second man, a Levite, did the same. I had always assumed that they did so because the rules for priests found in Leviticus 21:1–4 forbade them to make themselves unclean by touching a dead body. "Sorry, I have to stay pure. It's part of my job description."

But when I looked at a Jewish commentary regarding these purity regulations—which the legal expert in Jesus' day surely would have been familiar with—I found a surprise. The Jewish sages agreed that if a body is isolated and the victim has no one to bury him, then even the high priest has a moral obligation to care for the person and bury him with dignity, even if the act makes the priest ritually unclean. Not only that, but Jesus said that the priest and the Levite were on their way *down* to Jericho, perhaps for a little vacation? They could have purified themselves of any defilement before returning to work in the Temple. But of course, that would have interfered with their massage at the spa.

When both the priest and the Levite passed by on the other side, they might have appeared to be religiously correct, but they were far from the compassionate heart of God. The priests in Christ's day probably would have ignored the man, too, as they headed down to the hot springs, because in all of the New Testament stories that feature them, they seem greatly lacking in love: willing to stone the woman caught in adultery; following the letter of the Law but looking for loopholes around it; totally without compassion toward blind men or crippled women if their healing took place on the Sabbath. No wonder Jesus criticized a group of legal experts by saying, "You give a tenth of your spices . . . but you have neglected the more important matters of the law—justice, mercy and faithfulness" (Matthew 23:23).

Using the Law as an excuse to ignore a fellow human being in need is exactly what Jesus taught against when He accused the religious leaders of tying heavy loads on people's shoulders but not lifting a finger to help them; ignoring the commands of God to follow the traditions of men; straining the tiniest gnat out of their food because it wasn't kosher yet swallowing camels, the largest of the non-kosher animals. As Jesus told this story of a priest who looked the other way, the expert in the Law could not have missed the scathing condemnation of him and his fellow law-keepers.

It was a Samaritan, as much an enemy of the Jews as the modern-day Palestinians are, who acted with human kindness, going beyond mere obligation in caring for the wounded man. No law required him to do that. Acts of love and compassion can't be legislated. But helping someone in need was the loving thing to do, and he did it.

Jesus was saying that people need to stop following a list of rules and follow God's example of love and compassion. To truly love your neighbor, you must broaden your scope of who your neighbor is, even if it means helping your enemies. People like me want rules. We want to package God's laws in a neat set of books so that we can analyze them and reference them. If we do everything "by the book," we've done our duty. We want order and stability, the kind you find in a basketball game or a soccer match where we know all the rules and can clearly see when they're broken. We can cry "Foul!" and see the offender placed in the penalty box immediately. We want to know exactly whom to root for and who our enemy is. And we want our religion neatly structured, too, so we can keep score and know precisely what is required of us with no shades of gray in our black-and-white world.

Jesus broke the rules quite often, healing diseases on the Sabbath that were not life-threatening to deliberately show that a close, living relationship with God should serve as our guide, not rules. If the priest, the Levite, and the expert in the Law really knew the God they served, they would know that He is a "compassionate and gracious God, slow to anger, abounding in love and faithfulness, maintaining love to thousands, and forgiving wickedness, rebellion and sin" (Exodus 34:6–7). They would know exactly what their loving God meant when he said "Love your neighbor as yourself," without asking for a detailed description of precisely who their neighbor was. But their religion was out of balance, emphasizing the rules and missing the heart of God.

Jesus ended the parable with another question for the expert: "Which of these three do you think was a neighbor to the man who fell into the hands of robbers?" The only conclusion the expert could possibly reach was "The one who had mercy on him." It must have galled him to admit it, especially when Jesus added, "Go and do likewise."

A rich young ruler once asked Jesus the same question that the expert had asked: "What good thing must I do to get eternal life?" He assured Jesus that he had scrupulously followed all of the rules. Jesus told him to sell all of his possessions and give them to the poor—something the rich man couldn't bring himself to do. He loved something else more than he loved God or his neighbors in need (Matthew 19:16–30). The lesson isn't that I sell everything, too. It's that I look at my life and see if I put God first, giving all of my heart, soul, mind, and strength to Him. I need to ask myself if I'm living an outwardly correct life, playing by all the rules, but lacking in love. I need to see if I'm someone Isaiah and Jesus would include in their indictment, "These people honor me with their lips, but their hearts are far from me. They worship me in vain; their teachings are but rules taught by men" (Isaiah 29:13 and Matthew 15:8).

The priest in Jesus' story thought rules were more important than being led each moment by a living God, a God who wants us to open our eyes and see others in need and respond with compassion. The Hebrew word for priest, *Kohen*, means servant. The priests were servants of God and their fellowman. The New Testament tells us that we "are being built into a spiritual house to be a holy priesthood, offering spiritual sacrifices" (1 Peter 2:5). Are we becoming too "holy" to stop and help those who have been beaten up by the world and left for dead?

I also see this parable as a picture of Christ, "Who, being in very nature God . . . made himself nothing, taking the very nature of a servant" (Philippians 2:6–7). There is no uglier, sin-filled place than earth, filled with unclean, sin-scarred people. Yet Jesus left the holiness of heaven to cross over to our side of the universe and bind up our wounds at His own expense, restoring us to life. He showed us the heart of God. In turn, the way we view people in need reveals how Christlike we have become.

As our bus travels this modern Jericho road, I don't see any stranded, wounded travelers along the side of the road. But I think I now understand that my neighbor might have AIDS or live an immoral lifestyle or be a homosexual or a Muslim or an atheist. Will I stay far away from him, unwilling to associate with "defiled" people and become contaminated? Or will I show God's love and compassion wherever I encounter my neighbors in my everyday life, binding their wounds, giving

75

my own money, time, and resources for their care? There are Good Samaritans in this world who don't acknowledge God or follow His rules, yet they are eager to help the needy. Rock stars and celebrities raise millions of dollars to fight world hunger and AIDS and help victims of natural disasters. Why am I passing by on the other side?

But love your enemies, do good to them, and lend to them without expecting to get anything back. Then your reward will be great, and you will be sons of the Most High, because he is kind to the ungrateful and wicked. Be merciful, just as your Father is merciful.

Luke 6:35–36

A NEW PRAYER FOR THE JOURNEY

Gracious heavenly Father,
You are a God of love and compassion and mercy. I praise You for sending Your Son to our side of the road to heal our wounds and rescue us from death. Love is Your very nature, yet I confess that I haven't followed Christ's example of loving my enemies. Forgive me, Lord, for not standing at the crossroads and helping lost friends and loved ones find their way; for not being a better example of Your sacrificial love. Thank You for a new beginning in my life, a chance to climb out of my comfortable rut and journey with You on the road of discipleship, turning my back on the Good Life in pursuit of a godly life. Help me to embrace change with joy and faith, knowing that Your Spirit gives me the strength to conquer giants in Your name.
Amen

5

JERUSALEM

Great is the Lord, and most worthy of praise, in the city of
our God, his holy mountain. It is beautiful in its loftiness,
the joy of the whole earth.

Psalm 48:1–2

From my room in a nineteenth-century guesthouse inside the Old City walls, I awaken to the sound of bells
tolling at the Church of the Holy Sepulcher nearby. I
want to get an early start on this first day in Jerusalem, so
I bundle up against the cool morning air and sit outside on
our stone balcony to read my Bible. The trees in the open
courtyard below me rustle in the breeze, and the aroma of
our breakfast cooking in the guesthouse kitchen makes my
stomach rumble.

I settle back in my plastic chair and open to the Psalms.
When I see what today's psalm is, a thrill of excitement shiv-
ers through me. Psalm 48 celebrates Jerusalem as "the city
of our God, his holy mountain"—and that's where I am! I

know that God is everywhere and that I am never more than a prayer away from His presence, but Jerusalem is His city in a very historical, tangible way. It's where the Temple once stood, where Jesus was crucified, and where He rose again from the dead. Tears fill my eyes and blur the page as I read this psalm. I have been trying to find God's will among all of the changes in my life, and verses 12–14 offer me direction: "Walk about Zion, go around her, count her towers, consider well her ramparts, view her citadels, that you may tell of them to the next generation. For this God is our God for ever and ever; he will be our guide even to the end." Perhaps this pilgrimage is not only for my benefit, but so that I can bear witness to God's power and love "to the next generation" through my writing.

But my tears are for another reason, as well. This verse played an important role in my faith walk once before—one of those stones of remembrance in my life. More than twenty years ago when my children were still young, I struggled to discern God's calling for my life. I wanted to write. I loved to write. Yet how could I know for certain whether God wanted me to be a writer or if it was my own foolish idea? Were the hours I spent at the keyboard a waste of my time and God's?

Unsure, I decided to walk in faith in the direction I felt God was leading me, writing while my children napped, investing money and time in writing conferences to learn the craft, buying a computer so I could write more efficiently. Yet doubt plagued me. After hours of labor, I had not published a single word. My novel about the life of the Old Testament king Hezekiah remained unfinished. I longed to visit Israel and see the land I described in my novel, to study the culture and everyday life in biblical times. But as far as my writing was concerned, it seemed as though I would take one step forward and then slide two steps backward like a pawn in my children's Candy Land game.

Then God beckoned me to take a giant step forward, showing me an opportunity to volunteer on an archaeological dig in Israel for one month. I could take a college course in biblical backgrounds through Hebrew University, see the land, and research what ancient Israeli homes and villages might have looked like. But how would I afford such a trip? Our family lived in Canada at the time, and since I was a stay-at-home mom, the only moneymaking option for me was baby-sitting. Determined to go to Israel, I worked very hard for one very long Canadian winter, caring for my neighbor's three preschoolers in addition to my own three children, trying to save up enough money for the airfare. With my family's help and countless sacrifices, I managed to raise the funds. My husband cheered me on, encouraging me and offering to take over my duties at home so I could go.

Then, a few days before my trip, all three of my children became ill with chicken pox. That's when we discovered that my husband had never had chicken pox as a child. He had them now, and he was in misery. I felt like the captain of a plague ship as I scrambled to take care of everyone, soothing their fevers with aspirin, bathing them in lotion and tubs of warm water to ease the itching. I called the airline to see about changing my travel plans and learned that my charter ticket could not be rescheduled or refunded. All of the money that I had worked so hard to earn would be lost. Was this God's way of telling me that my plans had not been His? Several people from our church thought so. They telephoned to say that the chicken pox must be a sign from God that He wanted me to be a wife and mother, not a world-traveling writer. My husband, from his sickbed, disagreed. He said this plague was an attack from the enemy to make me doubt my calling. Who was right? Who should I believe?

I got on my knees and prayed, asking God for direction. Then I happened to open my Bible to my daily Scripture reading as I did every day. It was Psalm 48: "Walk about Zion, go around her, count her towers, consider well her ramparts, view her citadels, that you may tell of them to the next generation. For this God is our God for ever and ever; he will be our guide even to the end."

God had given me marching orders. He not only wanted me to go to Israel, but also to use my writing gift to tell of His faithfulness to the next generation. I listened to God and to my husband, not to the enemy's whispers, not to other people's opinions. I went to Israel and walked into my calling as a writer, in faith.

Now I'm in Jerusalem once again. In the intervening years, my five novels about the life of King Hezekiah have traveled the globe and been translated into languages as diverse as Indonesian, Romanian, Dutch, and Afrikaans. Readers all over the world write to tell me that my stories have made a difference in their lives. So why do I still doubt? Why do I find it so hard to believe that God has new things in store for me, life-changing things, if I put aside my fears as I did twenty years ago and embrace what He is asking me to do?

This morning in Jerusalem I've heard God speak to me again through Psalm 48. There are lessons for me here in the city of our God, lessons I shouldn't keep to myself but share. God invites not only me, but all of us to walk into His kingdom, to look around, to see what He has done and what He is doing, and then to find our purpose and calling in serving the next generation.

And so I lay aside my doubts and fears today and accept His invitation. I will walk around this city, view its ramparts and citadels, trusting that this pilgrimage will lead to the next great adventure that He has in store for me.

City Walls

The walls surrounding the Old City of Jerusalem are new compared to so many other artifacts in Israel, but I am still very impressed. Our guide says that Suleiman the Magnificent built them in the sixteenth century AD during the reign of the Ottoman Empire. It's easy to see by the stones' varied shapes and sizes that he recycled many of the building blocks from earlier walls, including King Herod's wall in the time of Christ. But the stones were all quarried from the same creamy golden limestone that makes Jerusalem a "city of gold." In some places along the wall's perimeter, the building blocks rest on enormous chunks of bedrock jutting above ground level. Suleiman originally built several gates into the city and stepping through one of them is like stepping into the past, into a maze of narrow, twisting streets, into a world of exotic spices and aromas. The guesthouse where we've been staying is inside these walls near the Jaffa Gate.

The massive walls of the Old City enclose an area of only .35 square miles, a space where the entire population of Jerusalem lived until 1860 when, for lack of room, Jewish settlers began building neighborhoods outside the walls. Jam-packed into this confined area are three important religious sites where the followers of the three monotheistic religions go to worship: the Church of the Holy Sepulcher for Christians, site of Calvary and the empty tomb; the Western Wall for Jews, a remnant of God's Holy Temple; and the Dome of the Rock for Muslims, the site where they believe the prophet Mohammed made his night journey into heaven. That's a lot of devotion to pack inside such a small space!

This morning, instead of exploring the Old City within the walls, we are getting an energetic workout as we try to circumnavigate the city on top of the walls. Whenever we reach a gate, we have to go down countless sets of stairs, cross to the other side of the gate, then climb up more stairs before continuing along the narrow walkway on top. But the panoramic view from the parapet makes the journey worthwhile as the newer sections of Jerusalem and the surrounding countryside lay spread out before us.

That view was one of the reasons why ancient peoples went to the trouble of building walls in the first place. If they could see their enemies approaching, they could quickly close and bar the gates. All available manpower would rush to the ramparts on the side of the city that was about to be attacked. Walls kept the enemy out and citizens safe inside.

Before the Israelites conquered Jerusalem, the Jebusites controlled the city. They thought their walls were impregnable, so they taunted King David, saying, "You will not get in here; even the blind and the lame can ward you off" (2 Samuel 5:6). They boasted too soon. David's men found the entrance to an ancient water system and climbed up the shaft to conquer the city. The archaeological excavations in the City of David have uncovered the ancient tunnel that David's men might have used.

I pause at a high point on the eastern rim of the wall and look down at the Kidron Valley far below. I can easily imagine the Old Testament King Hezekiah standing in this place on the wall, observing hundreds of thousands of Assyrian troops, the most powerful army on earth, encamped in the valley below him. They had already conquered all of Hezekiah's allies, and it looked like he would be next. The king did everything he could to prepare for the siege, reinforcing the walls and digging a tunnel and a reservoir to safeguard his water supply. I saw those preparations firsthand when I viewed a portion of Hezekiah's "Broad Wall" on display in the Old City.

Ultimately, it wasn't the walls that saved Hezekiah and Jerusalem, but God. Realizing his impossible situation, Hezekiah prayed for God's help, and "That night the angel of the Lord went out and put to death a hundred and eighty-five thousand men in the Assyrian camp. When the people got up the next morning—there were all the dead bodies!" (2 Kings 19:35). The most powerful army in the world was no match for God.

Courtyard Stairway

But Jerusalem's walls didn't stop the Babylonian army. Because of Israel's sin and idolatry, God allowed Babylon to conquer Jerusalem and carry the nation into captivity. After seventy years in exile, the Israelites returned to rebuild Jerusalem and the Temple. Nehemiah knew the value of protective city walls and took a leave of absence from his job as the Persian king's cupbearer to rebuild the walls around Jerusalem. Everyone in the city got involved in the project, and when Nehemiah's enemies tried to halt the work, he ordered the men to keep working and trust God. "Those who carried materials did their work with one hand and held a weapon in the other, and each of the builders wore his sword at his side as he worked" (Nehemiah 4:17–18). The walls, which were completed in only fifty-two days, not only made the people secure, but they also safeguarded God's newly rebuilt Temple, the nation's most valuable asset.

We've walked as far as we can go on our circuit of Jerusalem's walls and stand overlooking the plateau where the Temple once stood. The golden dome of the Muslim shrine dominates the paved square. Not even King Herod's fortified walls could stop the Romans from destroying Jerusalem and the Temple in AD 70. Israel went into exile a second time. Man-made walls can be toppled by man-made means, but God's rock of protection cannot be moved. God helped Nehemiah to rebuild the walls, David to conquer Jerusalem, and Hezekiah to remain safe because they all put their faith and trust in Him. But man-made walls didn't help the sinful Jebusites or a rebellious nation that had turned away from God.

So often, I'm tempted to build my own fortresses and rely on my own provisions for security. Money in the bank becomes my reservoir in times of drought. I trust my retirement plan to protect my future instead of seeing God as my security.

When I place my trust only in things that I can see with my eyes and touch with my hands, that's idolatry, whether I'm putting my faith in an engraved image or a savings account. Like Hezekiah and Nehemiah, I should remember that "God is our refuge and strength, an ever-present help in trouble. Therefore we will not fear, though the earth give way and the mountains fall into the heart of the sea" (Psalm 46:1–2). Or the stock market crashes. Or a tornado strikes. God never promised to protect me from all of my trials, but He did promise to be with me in the midst of them.

"Walk about Zion, go around her, count her towers, consider well her ramparts," the psalmist wrote—which is what I have been doing all morning—because the view will remind me how God rescued and saved His people in times past. But afterward, I need to tell "the next generation. For this God is our God for ever and ever." Each time I testify to God's faithfulness in my own life, it becomes a building block in my wall of faith and gives my children and future grandchildren something to stand behind. What a privilege to show the next generation that their own walls of faith can be carefully constructed by prayer and trust in One with a better view of the future than they have.

Whenever I'm tempted to lift up my eyes to the hills, looking for help from some other source, I want to remember that "My help comes from the Lord, the Maker of heaven and earth . . . the Lord will watch over your coming and going both now and forevermore" (Psalm 121:2, 8).

Hezekiah's Tunnel

The icy water takes my breath away. I wade into it, stepping down, and down again, until it reaches my thighs. But the shivery water isn't the worst part of this trek through King Hezekiah's tunnel. There is no light in here, electric or natural, and the claustrophobic tunnel meanders underground as if excavated by drunkards. Ahead of me, a tall man stoops to keep from smacking his head on the stone ceiling. A heavyset woman looks as though she regrets this adventure as she squeezes between the slimy walls. None of us can turn back. There's only enough room to walk single file.

This water system, deep below the city of Jerusalem, is man-made. The Bible tells us that "It was Hezekiah who blocked the upper outlet of the Gihon spring and channeled the water down to the west side of the City of David" (2 Chronicles 32:30). I know the story well. The first novel I ever wrote, *Gods and Kings,* was part of a three-book series about the life of King Hezekiah, who reigned in Jerusalem seven hundred years before Christ. With no supply of freshwater in the city and the vicious Assyrian army marching toward him, Hezekiah needed to find a way to safeguard the freshwater spring, located outside the city walls. His solution was to dig an underground tunnel from the spring to a new reservoir within the walls. Pressured to complete the work before the Assyrians attacked, he ordered the workers to start digging from opposite ends and meet in the middle.

"Hey, is it safe to trust a tunnel that was dug 2,700 years ago?" someone asks.

I shake my head, but no one sees me in the dark. No. I don't trust an ancient tunnel, especially in a city that has occasional earthquakes. I can only trust God—and splash forward, shining my feeble flashlight. The chiseled floor is uneven and rough, and since we can't see our feet below the inky water, we shuffle slowly, careful not to stumble and fall.

I'm not a big fan of caves, and this man-made one with its straight walls and squared-off ceiling is dark and creepy. The weight of the mountain above my head feels crushing.

"How much farther?" someone asks in a shaky voice. I don't dare tell her that this serpentine tunnel will wind for nearly a third of a mile and take about half an hour to walk through. The college students in our group try to lighten the atmosphere with laughter and jokes. Then one of them starts to sing: "Fill it up and let it overflow . . ." It's an upbeat version of "Amazing Grace" with an added refrain, "Fill it up and let it overflow, let it overflow with love." Soon, everyone joins in.

I smile to myself, remembering the first time I walked through Hezekiah's tunnel while researching my novel. Back then, my husband, Ken, and I were touring Israel with a group from our church in Canada, and the Palestinians had decided to start an *Intifada*—an uprising—while we were there. Hezekiah's tunnel had been on my "must-see" list, but Hillel, our tour guide, shook his head when I asked about visiting it.

"It is too dangerous to take a tour bus to that part of Jerusalem," he explained. "Yesterday the Palestinians attacked and burned a vehicle on the road that goes down to the tunnel. It is impossible to go there." Having come all the way to Israel to see Hezekiah's masterpiece, I was devastated. Late that night, wide-awake with disappointment and jet lag, I prayed, begging God to help me do the impossible.

The next morning I talked to the guide again, explaining about the book I was writing. Hillel finally agreed to take Ken and me through the tunnel by ourselves while the rest of the group toured another site. God had answered my "impossible" prayer.

Two days later, the three of us walked down the deserted road to the tunnel's entrance. When we passed the burned-out vehicle—an Israeli Army jeep—I nearly changed my mind and turned back. Were those bullet holes in the side of it? I nearly turned around again when we reached the tunnel's entrance and found that the gate, controlled by the Palestinians, was locked. But I decided I would trust God and keep going. He had brought me this far, hadn't He?

Hillel, who spoke Arabic, found someone to accept our "donation" and unlock the gate. Once inside, we discovered that I was the only one of us who had remembered to bring a flashlight. It was lipstick-sized and about as bright as a lightning bug's blink. Hillel would lead the way shining the light, and I would walk behind him clinging to his belt. Poor Ken would bring up the rear in near-total darkness, holding on to my shirttail and hoping that no one crept up behind him the way bad guys do in Saturday morning cartoons.

We descended the stairs and waded into the water. Within moments, the tunnel took a sharp turn and all outside light disappeared. My head skimmed the grimy ceiling, my shoulders scraped the walls. I could barely draw a breath as I sloshed through ice-cold water in suffocating darkness. Panic pumped through my veins. If Hillel hadn't gone to so much trouble to get me here—and if the restless Palestinians weren't waiting right outside—I would have turned around, trampled over Ken, and fled this awful place. But I shuffled forward, taking tiny baby steps, panting like an overheated hound on a hot day. Soon the water level passed my thighs and reached my hips.

"I-is it just my imagination," I asked, "or is this w-water getting deeper?"

"You're not imagining it," Hillel replied. "The little Arab children like to dam up the water when there are tourists inside, so that the tunnel will fill all the way up to our necks." *Fill it up and let it overflow!* I stopped walking. I could no longer breathe at all. We were trapped, with no way out! But then Hillel laughed out loud and told me he was only joking. "This water comes from a spring," he explained, "and it surges naturally every now and then." I would have pushed him underwater and drowned him, but he was clutching our only flashlight.

Now I join the students' song as I remember that first tour. The tunnel is less claustrophobic with more flashlights and more people. We reach the middle and stop to see the spot where the two tunnels met. Here, chiseled into the rock, was the oldest Hebrew inscription ever discovered, written by Hezekiah's men to explain how they had broken through after digging from opposite ends. The inscription is in a museum in Turkey, not here. We shine our flashlights on the wall and see where it once was, and also how the chisel marks slant from opposite directions at the meeting point.

This tunnel is an engineering marvel, especially when you consider that it was dug in 700 BC. Experts still aren't sure how anyone could dig two meandering tunnels that began a third of a mile apart and get them to meet up in the middle, deep underground. Impossible! Everyone who hears the story and sees the tunnel is impressed with King Hezekiah and his men.

But God wasn't impressed. He sent the prophet Isaiah to rebuke the king for all of his plans, saying, "You saw that the City of David had many breaches in its defenses; you stored up water in the Lower Pool. . . . You built a reservoir between the two walls for the water of the Old Pool, but you did not look to the One who made it, or have regard for the One who planned it long ago" (Isaiah 22:9, 11). In other words, Hezekiah was relying on his own preparations instead of trusting God.

Fifteen minutes later, a pinprick of light in the distance tells us we are almost to the end. I have a new respect for that old cliché about seeing the light at the end of the tunnel. I hear a lot of grateful sighs, including my own, when we wade out into the blinding sunlight. As we sit in the sun to warm up and let our clothes dry out, I'm still thinking of Hezekiah.

The city of Jerusalem was saved from the Assyrians, but not by this tunnel. When the most powerful army on earth surrounded Hezekiah, demanding surrender, he knew he'd reached the end of his resources. Facing an impossible situation, he went up to the Temple and knelt before God, placing his hope and trust in Him: "O Lord Almighty, God of Israel," he prayed, "You alone are God over all the kingdoms of the earth. . . . Now, O Lord our God, deliver us from [the enemy's] hand, so that all kingdoms on earth may know that you alone, O Lord, are God" (Isaiah 37:16, 20). That night, the angel of the Lord walked among the sleeping Assyrian warriors and put to death 185,000 of them. At dawn, the horrified king of Assyria gathered up his few surviving soldiers and bolted for home.

It's okay to make plans, but the lesson of Hezekiah's tunnel is that when we put our trust in God, not only is He victorious, but He is glorified. I think of the struggles I've experienced lately as life has veered out of my control, the times when I've panicked as the water has crept higher and higher until it seemed to reach my neck. In spite of all my feverish plans and schemes, the enemy has besieged and surrounded me, leaving me trapped with no way to escape. But as I sit in the sunlight outside Hezekiah's tunnel, I think of God's promise from Isaiah, the prophet in Hezekiah's time: "Fear not, for I have redeemed you; I have summoned you by name; you are mine. When you pass through the waters, I will be with you; and when you pass through the rivers, they will not sweep over you" (Isaiah 43:1–2).

We can step into the deep water, the darkness, the unknown—and trust God. At the end of the tunnel, we will emerge into dazzling sunlight.

The Pool of Siloam

At the end of Hezekiah's tunnel, in the oldest inhabited section of Jerusalem, we stop to rest at the Pool of Siloam. King Hezekiah built the original pool about seven hundred years before Christ to collect the runoff from his tunnel. But what I'm looking at now is the pool that existed in Jesus' day, recently unearthed by archaeologists. King Herod, that egomaniacal master builder, expanded the original Pool of Siloam to make it larger and grander, in the Roman style that he loved. Today, Herod's huge, public pool has been only partially excavated; it's dry and weed-filled and peppered with litter. But as we sit at what was once its edge and sip from our water bottles, the Pool of Siloam's former grandeur is evident nonetheless. About the size of a typical community pool, it was paved with creamy golden Jerusalem limestone. Wide stone steps on all four sides led gradually down into the refreshing spring water. An artist's rendering of the site shows crowds of well-dressed people wading in the clear water, lounging on the bleacher-like steps, and strolling in the shade beneath the pillared colonnade.

Jesus sent a blind man here to wash and regain his sight. As the man groped his way down the steps and into the water to splash the mud mixture from his eyes, his miraculous healing would have occurred before crowds of onlookers. For a rabbi who shunned publicity, Jesus seems to have chosen a very public place to send someone for a miracle—especially on the Sabbath. Once news of this miracle spread, I imagine a stampede of sight-impaired people rushing to the Pool of Siloam, thinking that the water was the source of the cure when the true source was Jesus.

This pool was part of a very important ritual during the Feast of Tabernacles, which included prayer for rain for the coming year. As crowds of worshipers followed and watched, a procession of robed priests drew water from the Pool of Siloam, then carried it up the hill to the Temple and poured it out around the altar. There the crowd listened in hushed silence as a priest read the prophecy of Zechariah, who had promised that living water would one day flow out from Jerusalem (Zechariah 14:8).

Imagine the priests' shock when, in the middle of this sacred ritual, Jesus suddenly stood up in a prominent place and interrupted the proceedings, shouting in a loud voice, "If anyone is thirsty, let him come to me and drink. Whoever believes in me, as the Scripture has said, streams of living water will flow from within him" (John 7:37–38). I wonder which made the priests angrier—the fact that Jesus disrupted their finely rehearsed ritual with His invitation, or that He dared to compare himself to living water?

"Living water" flows from a natural, God-given source such as a stream or a spring. Only living water may be used for ritual baths and purification ceremonies, which is why John baptized in a flowing river and why the priests drew water from the spring-fed Pool of Siloam. But Israel's leaders had rejected Jesus, the Living Water, and relied instead on their own lifeless rules and rituals for their righteousness. God told these leaders, "My people have committed two sins: They have forsaken me, the spring of living water, and have dug their own cisterns, broken cisterns that cannot hold water" (Jeremiah 2:13).

Cisterns are man-made holes, plastered and filled by hand. The water they hold is not "living." Cisterns must be patched and repaired and refilled or all the water will disappear. The loss might start with a small crack or a fissure; add on months of neglect and the water slowly trickles away. But a "living," moving source originates with our bountiful, life-giving God. Living water not only purifies; it doesn't run dry.

Our endless rushing and Pharisaical good works cannot bring righteousness any more than a ritual, without God, can bring rain. Any more than the Pool of Siloam, without Jesus, can bring healing. Yet we insist on using God as a magic charm, trying to do everything just right so our lives will be blessed. The Christian walk isn't about blessing, as I'm learning, but about a relationship—and that relationship is built and established with prayer. It's about obedience, even when I don't understand, even when it means a cross.

If I'm empty and dry, maybe it's because I have tried to satisfy my longings from man-made sources instead of allowing the Living Water to fill me. How foolish to expect a church service—with my preferred style of music, of course—to satisfy my soul when spiritual wholeness and healing come from a relationship with Christ, not a ritual. In my loneliness and loss, I have foolishly dug a lot of cisterns and started a lot of useless projects that eventually ran dry. But when my thirsty soul longs for water, my empty heart for healing, I can go to the true Source in prayer and be made whole. And God will freely give, never chastising me for trying to quench my own thirst.

I take another swig from my water bottle as I stare into the remains of the Pool of Siloam, and I can almost hear His invitation: "If anyone is thirsty, let him come to me and drink" (John 7:37). But Jesus said something else that day when He interrupted the carefully planned ceremony. He said, "Whoever believes in me, as the Scripture has said, streams of living water will flow from within him" (John 7:38). That means I'm also a source of living water.

We have an overflowing abundance of information and tools to help us in our Christian walk, a reservoir of religious freedom to draw from, yet we're often guilty of hoarding it in cisterns instead of letting it flow freely from us. We attend Bible studies and Sunday school classes year after year, storing up life-giving water but never sharing even a cup of it with others. Water that doesn't move becomes stagnant and dead, a breeding ground for mosquitoes and disease.

Living water that purifies the defiled, nourishes like a spring rain shower, and gives blind men their sight can't be hoarded. It needs to flow in and out. It needs to move through us, always flowing, ever changing. We need to be filled and refilled continually by Christ, the Living Water, not only for our own sakes, but so that streams of living water will flow from within us. So that we can say to a dying world, "Come, all you who are thirsty, come to the waters" (Isaiah 55:1). I am being refilled on this pilgrimage. Now it's time to let it overflow.

Yad Vashem

Our tour bus turns off the frenetic streets of modern Jerusalem and enters a peaceful park. Leaves rustle in the earth-scented breeze, birds twitter and chirp, the sounds of city life fade in the background. But the serenity becomes unsettling when we learn that we've entered the grounds of *Yad Vashem*, Israel's Holocaust memorial. The tranquility is that of a cemetery.

We leave the bus and walk along The Avenue of Righteous Gentiles, passing through a grove of trees planted in honor of people from all over Europe who risked their lives to rescue Jews from Hitler's "Final Solution." Each tree is marked with a plaque and a name, and I find trees for several of the heroes and heroines I've read about: Oskar Schindler, Dietrich Bonhoeffer, Raoul Wallenberg, and Corrie ten Boom.

I pause beside Corrie's tree to whisper a prayer of thanks. I read her book *The Hiding Place* when I was a young, newly married bride, and her true story made a lasting impression on me. Her life seemed so happy and ordinary in the beginning—much like my life back then with my new husband and my first teaching job—yet everything quickly changed for Corrie and her family after the Nazis occupied their country. Because of the Ten Boom family's deep faith in God, they made the decision to hide Jews in their home. The Nazis arrested Corrie, her father, and sister Betsie, and imprisoned them in a concentration camp. Corrie was the only survivor.

I wondered if I would have had the courage to do what she did. What would happen to my faith if I had to suffer because of it? Would I grow stronger as I leaned on God, or would I grow angry and lapse into despair if He failed to rescue me or answer my prayers the way I thought He should? Corrie's testimony brought me face-to-face with the shallowness of my faith, my lack of a deep relationship with God. Ken and I needed to build our new life together on a rock-solid foundation of prayer and faith and obedience. Corrie's book became a huge stepping-stone in my walk with God.

We leave the peaceful avenue and enter the museum. As visitors move from one end of the long, narrow building to the other, the exhibit tells the story of the Holocaust from its very beginning. The first thing we see is a towering wall that serves as a movie screen. Snatches of film from before World War II place us on a street somewhere in Europe. We're gazing through the windows of an apartment building, glimpsing everyday life in a Jewish community. We see families eating, working, worshiping; gathering for the Sabbath and singing songs that are as ancient as their faith; laughing, rejoicing, celebrating God. I shudder, knowing how it will end.

I turn and continue to walk, reading and studying the displays as I go. The museum floor slopes subtly down as I witness the gradual, ominous progression of hatred. It spews from public billboards and magazine pages and newspapers. The Nazis enact laws against Jews. They are fired from their jobs. Their homes and businesses are confiscated, looted. Jews are required to sew yellow stars on their clothing. They are ridiculed and harassed in the streets. As the persecution intensifies, desperate families gather their belongings and try to emigrate, only to find that few nations will take them.

Then comes *Kristallnacht*, "the night of broken glass," when 267 synagogues are burned, countless holy books destroyed, and hundreds of Jews beaten and killed in anti-Jewish riots. I'm struck by how "harmlessly" and gradually it all began before spiraling into genocide so violent that few people could have conceived of it, let alone believed it would happen. But the proof is in front of me, documented in photographs and on film and in stories told by survivors. As I walk and listen and read, the doorways to the exhibits become narrower, the rooms smaller and more confining until I find myself in the middle of a jumbled maze. I'm surrounded by images of Jews being rounded up at gunpoint and forced into ghettos and concentration camps. I've become separated from my husband and stuffed into a very tight space with strangers. Confused and disoriented, I search for the way out or the way that I came in, but I can't find either one. The lights are dim, the ceiling low. There are no windows.

I'm lost.

With nowhere to turn, I shuffle forward with the others and find that I'm being crammed into a railroad car like the ones that transported millions of Jews to their deaths. Claustrophobia sucks my breath away. I need to get out! Now!

As my panic builds, I realize that this fear and disorientation are exactly what the architect intended. I'm being forced to experience the same emotions that Jews felt as their joyful, song-filled world descended into a nightmare. I take deep breaths to control my panic and persevere through the maze, studying the horrific pictures. Death camps. Crematoria. Mass executions. Piles of discarded shoes and shorn hair and tattered suitcases, left behind by people whose lives ended in unimaginable horror. I look into the haunting faces of the men, women, and children who are slowly being driven to their deaths and my tears flow unchecked. For a few searing hours, I am experiencing a tiny taste of the Holocaust, and I can barely endure it. I want to run, but I can't escape. Neither could millions of Jews.

Slowly, the rooms become larger, the displays more orderly as the photos show Allied help arriving, bringing hope. The floor gradually slopes up again as I near the end. Hitler's forces retreat and surrender. The war ends. Salvation comes at last to survivors in the concentration camps and work camps. I see a photo of young Anne Frank, who longed to grow up and become an author like me, but who died of disease in the Bergen-Belsen concentration camp, six weeks before she would have been liberated.

The memorial of Yad Vashem ends with another towering wall on the opposite end of the building from the movie screen that depicted Jewish life before the Holocaust. This second wall is made of glass, and on the other side of it is a stunning view of modern Jerusalem. I look out at homes and apartment buildings with laundry fluttering from balconies. Mothers push baby carriages down sidewalks, young students hurry to catch a bus, old men sit around café tables. It's a view of treetops and hills and blue skies and streets pulsing with life. The prophet Zechariah might have envisioned this when he wrote these words about Israel's future: "This is what the Lord Almighty says: 'Once again men and women of ripe old age will sit in the streets of Jerusalem, each with a cane in hand because of his age. The city streets will be filled with boys and girls playing there . . . I will save my people from the countries of the east and the west. I will bring them back to live in Jerusalem; they will be my people, and I will be faithful and righteous to them as their God'" (Zechariah 8:4–5, 7–8).

I'm still weeping as we board the bus and drive away from the Holocaust memorial. I'm not alone in my tears. No one speaks as we each try to process what we've seen and experienced. Not only does the brutality of millions of deaths stun me, but also the realization that it occurred a mere decade before I was born. I think back ten years—and count forward ten years—and I shudder. This wasn't an event from the ancient past, enacted by primitive, superstitious people who didn't know any better. This happened in our modern era, among civilized nations. How quickly everything can change.

Yad Vashem raises terrible questions in my mind about why God would allow such atrocities, why He was silent in the face of so many Jewish pleas and prayers. We ask similar questions about His silence in the aftermath of hurricanes and earthquakes and tsunamis that take thousands of lives. Where is He? How can a loving God allow innocent people to suffer and die?

Grief-stricken by what I've experienced, I have no answers.

And yet God has offered an answer, if only we could comprehend it. He came down to this violent, hate-scarred planet in an act of unimaginable love to live among us and suffer what we suffer. The horror of Yad Vashem is only a taste of what Christ faced on the cross as He carried the weight of our most heinous sins. He not only endured torture and brutality, but He did it in love, so that even a Nazi officer could be forgiven if he bowed before Christ in repentance. God promises to be with us in our suffering even, as Corrie ten Boom and others have testified, if our suffering takes us to a lice-infested death camp.

The apostle Peter talks about the suffering we might face as followers of Christ and writes, "Dear friends, do not be surprised at the painful trial you are suffering, as though something strange were happening to you. But rejoice that you participate in the sufferings of Christ, so that you may be overjoyed when his glory is revealed" (1 Peter 4:12–13). I have never been persecuted for my faith or been forced to take a stand at the risk of my life. It's easy to be a Christian in America compared to Iran or China or Nazi Germany. It's easy to accept God's will for my life when it's one of abundance instead of persecution. So I ask myself the same question I asked after reading *The Hiding Place*: Would I fear the Nazis more than I feared God? Would I have chosen to follow Christ's example and love others at the cost of my own life, as Corrie and her family did?

As I am pondering all of these things, the bus travels across the city and arrives at the Jewish *shouk*. The colorful hubbub of this sprawling open-air market rouses me from my introspection. It's the eve of the Sabbath and the aisles and stalls are jammed with people haggling with shopkeepers, hurrying to finish their shopping before the day of rest begins. The sheer abundance of goods, the vibrancy of the colors and smells and sounds make it seem as though God is shouting, "Oh, taste and see that I am good!"

I wander through the market aisles past mounds of oranges, pistachios, avocados, and more varieties of olives than I've ever seen. I sample rich pastries still warm from the oven, gobbling several of my favorite chocolate-filled ones, licking melted chocolate from my fingers. Men in suits and ties purchase flowers and strawberries for their wives and special Sabbath treats for their children. Housewives greet each other with "Shabbat shalom," and leave carrying freshly baked *challah* bread and kosher wine. The bread and wine are Sabbath traditions and reminders, for me, of Christ's body and blood.

In another hour or two at sundown, all of this bustling activity is going to come to an abrupt halt. Businesses and workplaces will close, the market stalls will be shuttered, public buses will stop running. The day of Sabbath rest will begin, and God's people will pause to celebrate His goodness. Our suffering often causes us to turn away from God in anger. Here, His people still cling to Him—and He to them.

As unfathomable as the Holocaust still is to me, it's clear as I absorb the beauty and joy in this open-air marketplace that God has kept His promise to the children of Abraham. "This is what the Lord says, he who appoints the sun to shine by day, who decrees the moon and stars to shine by night . . . 'Only if these decrees vanish from my sight,' declares the Lord, 'will the descendants of Israel ever cease to be a nation before me'" (Jeremiah 31:35–36). Alongside Yad Vashem's portrait of mankind at our worst, I see a stunning portrait of our loving, promise-keeping God.

Jesus said that earthquakes, wars, and rumors of wars all will continue until He returns. In the meantime, life can change so quickly, as it did for Corrie ten Boom and for millions of Jews in Europe. For us, it might be the loss of a job, the unexpected death of a loved one, a life-shattering medical diagnosis, or a devastating tornado. Where am I placing my faith? Why do I cling to stuff that doesn't matter?

Whatever suffering we may endure, whatever the reason for the disasters we may witness, one thing is certain: our loving God remains sovereign over all of it. A few miles from Yad Vashem and this teeming, life-filled *shouk* is a hill called Calvary, where the battle against death has already been fought and won. "On this mountain he will destroy the shroud that enfolds all peoples, the sheet that covers all nations; he will swallow up death forever" (Isaiah 25:7–8). Christ's victory gives meaning to our present lives and hope for our future.

Therefore, my dear brothers, stand firm. Let nothing move you. Always give yourselves fully to the work of the Lord, because you know that your labor in the Lord is not in vain.

1 Corinthians 15:58

A New Prayer for the Journey

Almighty God and Father,
I praise You because Your sovereignty over this battle-scarred earth is never in doubt—and that sovereignty is always coupled with Your faithfulness and love. You are the Living Water, freely flowing, so that we will never thirst again. I look back at Your blessings to me in the past and ask Your forgiveness for trying to dig my own way out of the dark, dry places where You've put me. Forgive me for neglecting to build the walls of my relationship with You through prayer. Thank You that even our worst deeds and thoughtlessness can be forgiven in Christ, who suffered torture and death for my sake. Lord, please strengthen my faith as I look to You, and fill me with Your Living Water until I overflow to a thirsty world. Let all that I do be to Your praise and glory.
Amen

6

THE TEMPLE MOUNT

In the last days the mountain of the Lord's temple will be
established as chief among the mountains . . . and all nations
will stream to it. Many peoples will come and say, "Come,
let us go up to the mountain of the Lord, to the house of
the God of Jacob. He will teach us his ways, so that we may
walk in his paths."

Isaiah 2:2–3

I'm standing on an ancient paved street inside the walls of
Jerusalem's Old City. Above me is the hill where God's
Holy Temple once stood. The area all around me has
been made into an archaeological park, where tourists like
me can wander through ruins from Jesus' day. Back then,
this street probably resembled a busy urban shopping district
with swarms of people coming and going, ascending and
descending the immense staircases that led to the Temple on
the plateau above. It would have been especially busy during

the three yearly pilgrimage festivals when Jews came here to worship from all over the known world. I pass ruins of a row of shops like a modern strip mall, and I can almost hear the vendors hawking their wares and Jewish pilgrims haggling for a better price, as they still do in Jerusalem's open-air market.

Massive building stones and pillar sections now litter the ground, many of them hurled down from the Temple during its destruction by the Romans. Our guide points out the remains of support arches for a monumental stairway and bridge that once led up to the Temple's worship area on the top of the mount. The complex of Temple buildings and courtyards that stood above me in Jesus' day rivaled the Seven Wonders of the Ancient World. The statistics are mind-numbing and can't convey the magnificence of what pilgrims saw: a worship area that was twice the size of the Acropolis in Athens; a fifteen-story sanctuary adorned with billions of dollars' worth of gold; a courtyard the size of thirty football fields.

The Jews have long revered this mountain as the place where Abraham offered his son Isaac in obedience to God. "God himself will provide the lamb for the burnt offering," Abraham had said in faith, and God provided a ram caught by its horns, sparing Isaac (Genesis 22). To this day, the sound of a ram's horn is a reminder to the Jewish people of God's salvation. Archaeologists found an engraved stone from the Temple that reads "the place of trumpeting," marking the site on the pinnacle where the priests stood to blow their shofars.

King David purchased the Temple site for a permanent place of worship, and his son King Solomon built the first Temple here. The Babylonians destroyed it when they conquered Israel, but the Jewish exiles later rebuilt it in more modest proportions when their captors allowed them to return. Four hundred years later, King Herod decided that the Temple needed to be refurbished. He began an extensive reconstruction project here in 20 BC that was still ongoing in Jesus' day. Herod erected a huge retaining wall around the irregularly shaped mountain, backfilling it with earth and rocks and arched vaults to create a massive, level plateau on top that could accommodate a million pilgrims. The Romans destroyed Herod's Temple in AD 70, and I see the littered remnants of that demolition all around me: massive quarried stones, hundreds of pillar parts, carved columns, paving stones.

Some five hundred years after Christ, Emperor Justinian built the Church of St. Mary on the spot where the Temple once stood, but that was destroyed, as well. The mount is now home to an Islamic shrine, built around AD 690, with a golden domed mosque standing in the place where the Jewish Temple and the Christian church once stood. Muslims consider this the third holiest place in Islam, and access to the top is restricted and carefully controlled. I can only stand at the foot of the hill, surrounded by debris from the Temple, and gaze up, imagining what it might have looked like.

Herod's massive Temple project certainly impressed Jesus' disciples. "As he was leaving the temple, one of his disciples said to him, 'Look, Teacher! What massive stones! What magnificent buildings!' 'Do you see all these great buildings?' replied Jesus. 'Not one stone here will be left on another; every one will be thrown down'" (Mark 13:1–2). Jesus didn't see the buildings as they were but as they soon would become—not one stone left on another—which is how they look today. I picture Him shuddering as He spoke, the way I do when I see a photograph of the Manhattan skyline before 9/11 with the

Western Wall and Dome of the Rock on the Temple Mount

World Trade Center still intact. Superimposed over the towers in my mind are images I can never forget: airplanes crashing, flames and smoke billowing, steel structures crumbling like children's blocks. As Jesus looked ahead into Jerusalem's future, He saw death and destruction, too.

Herod's remodeled Temple was finally completed in AD 64, but it stood for only six years before the Romans demolished it. I can't comprehend the effort or the enmity that it took to hurl these huge building stones and pillar parts down from the top of the Temple mount, any more than I can comprehend the hatred that led to the destruction of the Twin Towers in New York. But Jesus was right, not one stone of the Temple sanctuary remains on another. His words must have seemed unbelievable to His disciples. But to make sure

Israel would recognize that the destruction was ultimately from God, Herod's Temple was destroyed on the ninth day of *Av*—the same day that Solomon's Temple was destroyed by the Babylonians in 586 BC. Jews still fast and pray to remember this twice-tragic day known as *Tisha B'Av*, one of the saddest days in the Jewish calendar year.

Jews are no longer allowed to worship on their Temple Mount. The Western Wall—or so-called Wailing Wall—where Jewish people pray, is not part of the original Temple structure but a remnant of the long retaining wall that Herod constructed around the mountain to form a plateau.

When the prophet Jeremiah warned about the coming destruction of Solomon's Temple by the Babylonians, the religious leaders had him arrested, saying, "This man should be sentenced to death because he has prophesied against this city" (Jeremiah 26:11). Jeremiah's life was spared, but the Temple wasn't, just as he'd predicted. Jesus warned that Herod's Temple also would be destroyed, and Jesus' enemies, like Jeremiah's, sought to execute Him for it, twisting and misinterpreting His words, "Destroy this temple, and I will raise it again in three days" (John 2:19).

I look at this jumble of stones, and they sober me. If Jesus was right about this seemingly impossible feat of destruction, why don't I pay closer attention to His other warnings? In speaking about the Day of Judgment and the end of the age, He said, "Because of the increase of wickedness, the love of most will grow cold" (Matthew 24:12). *Most.* He warned, "Be careful, or your hearts will be weighed down with dissipation, drunkenness and the anxieties of life, and that day will close on you unexpectedly like a trap. For it will come upon all those who live on the face of the whole earth. Be always on the watch, and pray" (Luke 21:34–36). Am I as guilty as the people who heard Jesus and Jeremiah and ignored their warnings? If America had been forewarned about the 9/11 attacks, wouldn't we have taken them seriously? How should we live now, with Jesus' warnings in view?

Jesus said that wickedness would increase, which is not hard to imagine when I look at our modern world. But more worrisome for me, He predicted that our love will grow cold, meaning our love for God and for others. After forty-two years of marriage, my husband and I work very hard to continually refresh our relationship, taking care that our love doesn't grow cold. One key we've discovered is to spend time together and not allow busyness to interfere. How much more important, then, to put time and effort into my relationship with God and keep my spiritual passion alive after nearly fifty years as a professing Christian? Jesus warned the believers in Ephesus, "You have forsaken your first love" (Revelations 2:4). I don't want that to be true of me. If my husband and I plan periodic date nights, surely I can take time out for prayer and for periodic spiritual retreats—a "date night" with God.

Not only should I tend the flames of my passion for God, I also should make certain that my love for others doesn't grow cold. Experts talk about "compassion fatigue," which occurs when we become overwhelmed by trying to meet the needs of people affected by natural disasters, such as earthquakes and floods. We simply can't absorb one more catastrophe, and we begin to numb ourselves to people's pain, like a shot of emotional Novocain. Am I guilty of that?

I need to examine my interactions with others to make sure I'm not so wrapped up with my own concerns that I forget to reach out. Our church is addressing this problem by planning a local mission project right in our own community. Church members of all ages will tackle work projects for elderly neighbors who need a hand and help local families who need assistance in our depressed economy. It should be a priority for me to be part of that outreach. Again, expressing love seems to be measured in terms of spending time and not necessarily money.

Jesus ends His warning with these words: "Be always on the watch, and pray" (Luke 21:36). The foundation stone of every marriage is communication, taking time to talk to each other, listen to each other, share our joys and needs and worries. It's the heart of our love relationship with God, too. Jesus often went to a quiet place to be alone with His Father in prayer. I know how important prayer is. Yet I've allowed my worries to distract me instead of drawing me to God. In my anger and disappointment, I've given God the "silent treatment," just as I'm sometimes guilty of doing with my husband. I'm grateful for the time I have on this pilgrimage to begin sharing my worry and grief and fear with Him in prayer once again, grateful for the time to listen to what He's saying to me in reply. I'm laying the foundation for a better prayer life when I return home.

This ancient, bustling street in Jerusalem is now deserted, the shopkeepers and customers long gone. But the jumbled pile of building stones that once were part of the Temple also give me hope. Jesus said, "I am coming soon. Hold on to what you have, so that no one will take your crown. Him who overcomes I will make a pillar in the temple of my God. Never again will he leave it" (Revelation 3:11–12).

I want to be a pillar in the new Temple that Jesus has begun to build.

Living Stones

I climb up the sweeping set of stairs below the Temple Mount, but they are steps to nowhere. They once led to a set of doors in the Temple's massive retaining wall and to an enclosed stairway that led to the top. But the doors have been bricked shut. If I look where the guide is pointing, I can see the outline of the ancient doors from the time of Christ and part of a stone lintel above the doorframe. At the top of the steps, I pose for a photograph beside one of the retaining wall's original building stones, an enormous block at least eight feet long and four feet high. It must weigh several tons, yet the masons cut each stone so perfectly that no mortar was necessary to hold it in place. Directly below me are the remains of several *mikvoth*, the ritual baths where worshipers immersed themselves to become ritually clean before offering their sacrifices.

These stairs and doorways served as one of the main entrances to the Temple complex, leading worshipers up from street level to the top of the mount, high above me. Jesus climbed these same smooth limestone steps to reach God's House. I wish I could follow Him through the now-closed doorway into the shadowy darkness, then up the enclosed stairs. We would emerge into brilliant sunlight on the vast, paved square above and see God's dazzling Temple, glittering with gold.

Jesus walked here. I shiver as I look out at the same view He would have seen as He stood in this spot, with the Mount of Olives across the valley to our left and the City of David below us. The modern city may look different and the Temple is no longer above us, but the mountains and valleys and skies look the same as they did to Jesus. Pilgrims who come to Israel to walk where Jesus walked are often bewildered to find themselves viewing gaudy churches. But these stairs and the view from the top of them are authentic.

The doors and enclosed stairway have been sealed shut for centuries. But for those of us who know Christ, we no longer need a temple to offer our sacrifices because "we have been made holy through the sacrifice of the body of Jesus Christ once for all" (Hebrews 10:10). Even so, God has never been without His Temple. "Don't you know that you yourselves are God's temple and that God's Spirit lives in you?" the Scriptures ask. "God's temple is sacred, and you are that temple" (1 Corinthians 3:16–17). God began building this new temple on the Jewish Feast of Shavuot, the second required pilgrimage festival, fifty days after Passover, fifty days after Jesus rose from the dead. We call it the Day of Pentecost.

Imagine the disciples as observant Jews, gathering together as a group after the resurrection to celebrate the Feast of Shavuot. On this day, worshipers would bring the very first fruits of their summer crops to the Temple in a joyful procession. They had tied ribbons on those offerings back home as soon as the fruit first appeared in the spring, marking them for God. The day also commemorates the giving of the Law on Mount Sinai and is remembered by a public reading of the Torah. On the very first Shavuot, when Moses returned from the mountain with the Ten Commandments, three thousand Israelites died in punishment for worshiping the golden calf.

As Jesus' disciples and followers began their celebration at nine o'clock in the morning, something amazing happened. "Suddenly a sound like the blowing of a violent wind came from heaven. . . . All of them were filled with the Holy Spirit" (Acts 2:2, 4). In the Old Testament, God's Holy Spirit came in small doses, resting for a limited time on His prophets and others anointed for His work. But God promised that one day "I will pour out my Spirit on all people . . . even on my servants, both men and women" (Joel 2:28–29). Now it had happened. All of them were filled with the Holy Spirit's power. When people came running to see what was going on, Peter preached to the amazed crowd of Jews who had come from all over the world for the feast. Three thousand people were baptized that day and became followers of Christ, the firstfruits of His worldwide body.

Many scholars believe that the events of Pentecost took place here at the Temple. Scripture says that the wind "filled the whole house where they were sitting," and Jews typically called the Temple "The House" (Acts 2:2). Unlike Passover, which is celebrated in private homes, Pentecost was celebrated at the Temple, so it's likely that Peter and the others would want to gather there early in the morning on this important feast day. Besides, a typical Jewish home in Jerusalem would have been much too small to accommodate a speech to three thousand people. These steps leading to the Temple's main entrance would have made a wonderful stage and bleachers for the event. And the ritual baths directly below me would provide a convenient place to baptize three thousand new believers.

But the location of Peter's Pentecost speech isn't important. What's important is that on this day, God set the first stones of His new Temple in place. "You are . . . built on the foundation of the apostles and prophets, with Christ Jesus himself as the chief cornerstone. In him the whole building is joined together and rises to become a holy temple in the Lord. And in him you too are being built together to become a dwelling in which God lives by his Spirit" (Ephesians 2:19–22). God sent His Holy Spirit to dwell not in a man-made building, but in His people. A temple built of enormous stone blocks doesn't have the ability to "Go into all the world and preach the good news to all creation" (Mark 16:15). But this new temple, like the original tabernacle that Moses built in the wilderness, can travel wherever God commands His people to go.

I don't always realize until I stand here what a privilege we have. For centuries, God's Spirit was thought to dwell only here in His Temple. But now the Holy Spirit dwells in us. I can leave this place and He goes with me, guiding me, shaping me. "And surely I am with you always," Jesus promised, "to the very end of the age" (Matthew 28:20). But with that promise comes responsibility.

I look up at these remaining stones from the Temple's retaining wall and see how perfectly the masons cut each huge stone to fit in its exact place. It's a picture of us as His "living stones." Peter wrote, "As you come to him, the living Stone—rejected by men but chosen by God and precious to him—you also, like living stones, are being built into a spiritual house" (1 Peter 2:4–5).

The phrase *living stone* has a double meaning. We are obviously alive with beating hearts and living bodies, and we have the life of Christ in us. But a *living stone* is also a technical term used to describe a rock that has been quarried, cut, and shaped into a building block. Lately, I have felt like a rock in a quarry as I've experienced cutting and chipping and painful carving. But when I look up at the Temple wall's original building stones, standing firmly in place without mortar for two thousand years, I can begin to imagine what the final result will be when God's work in me—and in us—is finished.

The Greek word that describes Jesus as a carpenter means much more than someone who works exclusively with wood. It means a master builder or a stone mason—and visitors to Israel quickly see that the majority of buildings here are made of stone, not wood. Jesus, our master builder, can use the painful trials we experience to cut and shape us for our perfect place in His new temple. If we allow Him to work, we become "living stones," shaped to fit tightly together, shoulder to shoulder. We are the Temple of God, shining like millions of dollars' worth of gold. How comforting to know that all of the pain we experience now, when surrendered to Him, will one day bring glory to God.

If I resist His work in my life, I become as useless as a block in a stair that leads nowhere, facing a dead end. But shaped by Christ's grace and love, I become a stepping-stone to help people find their way up out of the darkness into God's dazzling light.

The Kotel

Today I am going to the Jewish place of prayer, the Western Wall. The Israelis call it simply the *Kotel*—The Wall—and it is one of Judaism's holiest sites. This section of what was once King Herod's retaining wall is the closest point to where the Temple sanctuary stood on the plateau above. The sanctuary housed the Holy of Holies and the ark of the covenant. It was God's dwelling place on earth.

Thousands of people come to worship here at the Kotel every day, but to get here we have to pass through a security checkpoint guarded by Israeli soldiers. Women must have their purses and bags searched, men must empty their pockets and open their backpacks. Everyone must pass through a metal detector. I see soldiers everywhere, some watching us from high above the Kotel. I'm told that security intensifies on holidays.

Once we're past the gates, sunlight fills the spacious, open-air plaza. Men and women worship separately, just as they did in God's Temple, with a low barrier dividing the two areas. I go to the women's side and approach the wall, looking up at the massive stone blocks, some as large as three feet high and six feet long, rising several stories above my head. I feel a sense of joy and awe. Some of the women, unwilling to turn their backs on this holy site, walk backwards as they leave the wall, their hands folded in prayer.

I have followed the tradition of writing my prayers on a scrap of paper to tuck into one of the narrow cracks between the stones. Hundreds of such prayers already cram every available space. I push my paper between the blocks, then close my eyes and pray. The stones feel sun-warmed as I rest my hand against the wall. For some reason I am overcome with emotion. I know I can pray anytime, anywhere, but there is a sense of accumulated faith here, as if the prayers of countless millions of worshipers throughout the centuries still linger in the air.

When King Solomon first dedicated the Temple a thousand years before Christ, he prayed these words: "As for the foreigner who does not belong to your people Israel but has come from a distant land . . . when he comes and prays toward this temple, then hear from heaven, your dwelling place, and do whatever the foreigner asks of you, so that all the peoples of the earth may know your name and fear you" (2 Chronicles 6:32–33). Three thousand years ago, Solomon prayed for me!

I gaze up at this fortress-like wall when I finish praying and try to hold on to the feeling I have. I want to envision God as my Rock, my Fortress, as strong and protective as this towering wall. I want to remember that I can fold up all of my needs and prayer requests and place them in His care, then walk away and leave them, knowing He has heard me.

I follow the other women's examples and slowly back away from the wall. After rejoining my group, I make my way across the plaza and exit the secure area, passing long lines of people waiting to enter through the checkpoint. It seems incongruous to me to submit to an inspection on the way to worship or pray, but without security measures, the Kotel would become a prime target for Israel's enemies.

The Jews in Jesus' day were as zealous for the holiness of the Temple as the modern security guards are for its safety. The largest area of the Temple Mount, the Court of the Gentiles, was open to all worshipers. But only Jews could go beyond the barriers into the Court of Women or the even smaller Court of Men—provided they were ritually clean, that is, and not blemished or crippled. A large sign warned that any non-Jew who tried to worship in these inner courtyards would be put to death. The apostle Paul was nearly killed in a riot at the Temple because the Jews believed he had brought a Gentile from Ephesus named Trophimus into this sacred area (Acts 21:27–36).

Beyond the court for Jewish men, access to the Temple continued to become more and more restricted. Only ordained priests and Levites could approach the altar to offer sacrifices. Only they could enter the Temple sanctuary itself and burn incense or light the menorah in the Holy Place. And the holiest chamber of all, the Most Holy Place, separated from the rest of the sanctuary by a curtain, was off-limits to everyone except the High Priest—and he could enter only once a year on the Day of Atonement, bearing the blood of the sacrifice. Imagine the priests' horror on the day of Christ's crucifixion when, at the moment of Jesus' death on the cross, "the curtain of the temple was torn in two from top to bottom" (Matthew 27:51). Christ had opened a direct path to God for everyone who accepted His sacrifice on the cross, men and women, Jews and Gentiles.

Jesus zealously guarded the sacredness of the Temple but not for the same reasons that the priests did. In His day, the Court of the Gentiles had been turned into a loud commercial shopping mall where money changers had set up shop and sacrifices were sold. People even used that courtyard as a shortcut to carry merchandise from one side of Jerusalem to the other. If any foreigners like me came to worship, as King Solomon foresaw, they had to fight their way past the animal stalls and noisy bartering marketplace to find a place to pray. Jesus turned all the tables upside down, quoting the prophets Jeremiah and Isaiah as He tossed aside crates of doves and bags of money to cleanse the courtyard. "Is it not written: 'My house will be called a house of prayer for all nations'? But you have made it 'a den of robbers'" (Mark 11:17). Jesus cleared the way so that everyone who sought the God of Israel could have access to Him.

I want to take a careful look at my place of worship back home with this in mind. What can I do to make sure that our church sanctuary provides an atmosphere of reverent awe and worship? Is it sanctified as a holy place where nothing profane is allowed to desecrate it and detract from worship? Is it a place where both believers and seekers can come and truly worship our Holy God, or has it become a busy, babbling marketplace?

Maybe I should set up a security checkpoint around my own worship times, too. Whether praying at home or in church, I need to keep all of my enemies out, including my own distracting thoughts, petty complaints, and the weight of stored grievances that hang on my shoulders like a bulging purse. If my worship feels stale, maybe it's because my barriers are down, and I'm allowing unwelcome distractions to enter.

On Sundays, the enemy seems to know just how to make sneak attacks on my husband and me so we'll arrive at church grumpy and out of sorts, hardly in a mood to worship. We need to go through a spiritual checkpoint so we can come with a right attitude and a forgiving heart if we would like God's forgiveness. Jesus said, "Therefore, if you are offering your gift at the altar and there remember that your brother has something against you, leave your gift there in front of the altar. First go and be reconciled to your brother; then come and offer your gift" (Matthew 5:23–24). What if I took a few moments to prepare my heart and mind ahead of time to worship? The same is true of my quiet times at home. Before meeting with a Holy God, I could turn off the incessant mind-chatter, the distracting telephone and email alerts, cleansing the courtyard as Jesus did.

I'll always remember the awe I felt today when praying at the Kotel—and also the joy I saw on the other worshipers' faces. Worship and prayer are ways to approach a holy, righteous, and gracious God who is waiting to meet with us. The curtain of separation has been torn in two, and we can feel the warmth of His love—like sun-warmed stones—anytime and in any place.

Bar Mitzvah

I have returned to the Kotel to pray. There is something about the Wall that draws me, a sense of holiness and connection as I remember all of the men and women from Scripture who have worshiped here, all of my favorites like Isaiah and King Hezekiah and Jeremiah and, of course, Jesus. Today I hear drums and cymbals and music, the trumpeting of shofars, sounds of a joyful celebration. Excitement fills the air as musicians in gold-trimmed white robes lead a procession across the plaza to the Kotel, escorting a young boy beneath a portable, velvet-draped canopy. Visitors turn to watch as the musicians usher him and his family to the Wall with singing, clapping, rejoicing. The boy looks a little sheepish, as if unaccustomed to being the center of attention among his family and friends—much less being stared at by hundreds of strangers and tourists taking photographs.

Today is the boy's *bar mitzvah* celebration. Today he becomes a "son of the commandment," which is what the words *bar mitzvah* mean in Hebrew. He will have the honor of reading the daily Torah passage aloud to the others, and he can take his turn reading Scripture in the synagogue from now on. He will wear phylacteries on his forehead and arm for the first time today, and then for the rest of his life when he prays each morning. These small boxes, which fasten to his forehead and left arm by leather straps, contain passages of Scripture from Exodus and Deuteronomy. Jewish men are commanded to "Tie them as symbols on your hands and bind them on your foreheads" (Deuteronomy 6:8).

I watch as the young man's procession makes its way inside the worship area near the Wall. The men in his family surround him while the women and young girls watch from behind the low barrier, showering him and each other with candy. The psalmist declared, "How sweet are your words to my taste, sweeter than honey to my mouth!" (Psalm 119:103). The candy helps children associate God's Word with sweetness from the time they are very young.

The Bible says that "Every year [Jesus'] parents went to Jerusalem for the Feast of the Passover. When he was twelve years old, they went up to the Feast, according to the custom" (Luke 2:41–42). At age twelve, boys in Jesus' day became responsible for celebrating the Jewish feasts as adults, and this was likely the first time that Jesus would get to study and read the Torah with the other men in preparation for His own bar mitzvah. "Everyone who heard him was amazed at his understanding and his answers" (Luke 2:47).

The study of Scripture was of such importance to Jesus that He lingered behind in Jerusalem when the festival ended instead of joining His family for the trip home. I can understand if a child wants to stay behind at Disney World, but how many children would choose to stay in a place of worship to study the Bible with their elders? When Jesus' worried parents finally found Him, He said, "Why were you searching for me? Didn't you know I had to be in my Father's house?" (Luke 2:49). In these few, brief verses, we get a sense of His love for His Father's Word and His eagerness to read and study it.

I picture twelve-year-old Jesus looking much like this modern-day bar mitzvah boy with his dark hair and eyes, surrounded by his proud, doting family. Like this boy, Jesus would have worn a head covering, or *kippah*, while praying, and His mother would have sewn tassels called *tzitzit* to the corners of His garments, as the Torah commanded. He probably wore phylacteries on His forehead and arm when He prayed every morning. We know that devout Jews wore them in Jesus' day because He admonished the Pharisees for making a show of them. "Everything they do is done for men to see: They make their phylacteries wide and the tassels on their garments long" (Matthew 23:5). But Jesus never said Jews shouldn't wear them at all. These symbols on forehead and arm reminded Jews to keep God's commands in the forefront of their minds and let them guide all of their actions.

Watching the bar mitzvah festivities makes me long for a rite of passage to celebrate our decision to become men and women of God's Word. If only we had Jesus' passion to study Scripture, to consider God's Law sweeter than honey, and to read it with joy instead of as just another item on our to-do list.

The Jewish way of studying the Bible is very different from ours. In the Sunday school classes and Bible studies that I've attended or taught, many Christians seem afraid to ask the hard questions, afraid of sounding like a heretic—or worse, afraid that the answers or lack of answers might topple the shaky walls of our faith. For example, how do we reconcile "Thou shalt not kill" with God's command to Joshua to slaughter every Canaanite man, woman, and child? How does the Bible's clear statement that "the Lord your God is One" fit with our doctrine of the Trinity? So we decide not to dig too deeply, sticking to the pat answers that we've been taught. Too many of our teachers stand in front of our young people and say, "This is what you need to know; this is what this Bible passage means; these are the lessons we can learn from the story of David and Goliath or Noah's ark." We package everything neatly as if God can fit on a flannel board, making sure our children always color between the lines on their activity pages. We're content when our students can echo back everything we've said and overjoyed if they profess to us that they believe every word of it.

In Jewish teaching, questions are the essence of the way young people learn. Their teachers pose a hard question, knowing that the Jewish sages themselves don't always agree on the answer. Back and forth the students fly from one verse of Scripture to the next, digging into what each one says, studying how each contradiction shines a tiny bit of light on the problem. Confused about a particular word, they'll find the first place in the Torah where that word is used and examine the context for answers. That, I believe, is what Jesus and the teachers at the Temple were doing that day. "Everyone who heard him was amazed at his understanding and his answers." The teachers would have asked questions that the wisest sages in Judaism had discussed and argued about since the time of Moses. They weren't expecting pat answers from these young Torah students, a 100 percent on the quiz. But Jesus would have revealed to them from Scripture what God's Word really, truly meant. Not only were the elders astounded, but Jesus was having fun—like a trip to Disney World.

The way to deepen our children's faith isn't to give them milk but meat to chew on. And the way to do that is to be brave enough to ask the tough questions. My first wrestling match with God some thirty years ago didn't destroy my faith; it made me read the Bible, searching, asking, digging. I tried to teach my children that whenever they have doubts and fears it's okay to wrestle with God the way Jacob did. That's what Jacob's new name, Israel, means: the people who struggle with God.

When my daughter Maya was fourteen and first felt called to minister to the Jewish people, she discovered an inconsistency in Christian practice. Maya had celebrated Passover with one of her Jewish friends from school and recognized all of the beautiful pictures of Christ in the Passover Seder. She also saw that the Last Supper was a celebration of that same Passover meal, and so when Jesus took the bread and broke it, saying, "This is my body," He used unleavened bread. She had been taught from Scripture that leaven is a type of sin . . . one small pinch of it destroys our entire body the way a tiny pinch of leaven raises an entire loaf of bread. She then asked the question—no, she demanded to know—why did our church use leavened bread for Communion? Why did our ministers hold up loaves of leavened bread when they said, "This is Christ's body, broken for you." Christ was without sin. Our church should use unleavened bread.

She was right, of course. I told her to ask her youth leader. He shrugged and suggested she ask the church elders. The next time we had Communion she marched into the vestry when they were preparing the Communion plates and asked why they were using leavened bread. Most of them laughed it off, made a joke of it. One of them said it was tradition, the way it had always been done. Another said that grocery stores in our town didn't sell the unleavened kind. In reply, she named the aisle in our local supermarket where her Jewish friends had purchased unleavened bread for Passover.

Not content to have her honest question brushed aside, Maya asked our senior pastor. To his credit, he didn't dismiss her with a pat reply. Instead, he promised to think about it and get back to her. When he did, he also saw the beautiful significance of unleavened bread—naturally striped and pierced—as a type of Christ's body. At our next Communion service, he gave a lengthy explanation of why, from now on, unleavened bread would be in the Communion plate, not the traditional kind. He also fielded countless complaints from members of the congregation for daring to change the traditional way of doing things.

I was proud of my daughter and her willingness to ask hard questions, as proud as these bar mitzvah parents must feel. As she grew, her questions weren't always as successfully and fully answered as they were in this case. She stirred a lot of angry hornets' nests in the Christian college she attended and is doing it now in her studies at the college in Jerusalem. But her faith remains strong enough not to be shaken by difficult questions.

I believe the Jewish way is so much wiser. If we don't allow our children to ask, if we don't encourage them to ask, they are going to ask nonetheless—but they won't be equipped to look for the answers in Scripture. We'll make them feel guilty and sinful and un-Christian for doubting, reluctant to show any chinks in their armor of belief. We know they must have doubts—we all do, if we're honest. The Jewish way is to keep digging, keep asking, tearing the Bible apart line by line, knowing that God will show us the answer if we search with all our heart. None of us should be content with pat answers or God-in-a-box theology. This pilgrimage has already strengthened my flabby spiritual muscles as I've wrestled with God.

The bar mitzvah ceremonies continue as I leave the Kotel. Later, the boy's family will celebrate with a feast to mark his entrance into the study of Scripture. We may not have a rite of passage like the bar mitzvah, but God still wants us to grow up and put away childish things, to become sons and daughters of His Word. Jesus said, "Until heaven and earth disappear, not the smallest letter, not the least stroke of a pen, will by any means disappear from the Law" (Matthew 5:18). That means He wants us to know it, study it, cherish it. And above all, rejoice in the sweetness of it.

> And I heard a loud voice from the throne saying, "Now the dwelling of God is with men, and he will live with them. They will be his people, and God himself will be with them and be their God."

> Revelation 21:3

A NEW PRAYER FOR THE JOURNEY

Our loving heavenly Father,
You are our strong tower of protection, the One we can run to for refuge. Yet You are always with us wherever we are, close enough to hear our whispered prayers. Forgive me for letting my love for You and for others to grow cold; for allowing time or anger or distractions or anything else to keep me from drawing near to You in prayer. Forgive me for resisting the Stonemason's chisel as You have sought to use my struggles to shape me into a living stone for Your new Temple. Thank You for giving us Your Living Word in Christ to remove the barriers between us and You. And thank You for Your written Word, Your love letter to us that teaches us how to love You, serve You, and live for You. Please renew my love of Scripture, the challenge of it, the sweetness of it. Help me to take my place as a living stone—for Your sake and for Your glory.
Amen

7

HOLY WEEK

O Jerusalem, Jerusalem, you who kill the prophets and stone
those sent to you, how often I have longed to gather your
children together, as a hen gathers her chicks under her wings,
but you were not willing.

Matthew 23:37

Wild rosemary and sage perfume the early morning air as I lace on my walking shoes. Today will be a day of vigorous hiking as we retrace Jesus' footsteps in the week leading up to Easter Sunday. I gulp down my tea, shake off my drowsiness, and ride the bus to the sleepy village of Bethany, home to Mary, Martha, and Lazarus.

The insignificant town where Jesus raised Lazarus from the dead is about two miles from Jerusalem as the crow flies. It seems much farther as our bus drives up and over the Mount of Olives, navigating the labyrinth of narrow, traffic-packed streets. But Bethany was close enough to Jerusalem for word of Jesus' miracle to fly there faster than a carrier pigeon. The miracle became the fuel that turned His enemies' smoldering anger into a fiery determination to kill Him: "Many of the Jews who had come to visit Mary, and had seen what Jesus did, put their faith in him. But some of them went to the Pharisees" (John 11:45–46). The high priest, Caiaphas, decided that "it is better for you that one man die for the people than that the whole nation perish" (v. 50). "So from that day on they plotted to take his life" (v. 53).

The village of Bethany was probably just as small and tightly packed back then as it is now. Of course, a church sits on top of Lazarus' tomb today. I file down a creepy set of narrow, stone stairs below it to see the underground tomb. It's claustrophobic down here, worthy of a good horror film. I'm as glad to get out as Lazarus must have been.

When our visit to Bethany is finished, we set out on foot for the two-mile trek to Jerusalem, just as Jesus and His disciples did on Palm Sunday. I live in the American Midwest, where a two-mile walk along a flat prairie trail takes little time and not too much effort. But Jerusalem sits on a mountaintop with even bigger mountains surrounding it like beefy bodyguards. To reach Jesus' destination at the Temple, we need to climb uphill to the top of the Mount of Olives, down the other side to the Kidron Valley, and then up again to the top of Mount Moriah. In Scripture, Jesus and His disciples seem to take these hills in stride. The Bible never mentions anyone huffing and puffing the way I am. No one complains or says, "Hold up while I catch my breath!" I hope my physical condition isn't a reflection of my spiritual state.

One-third of the way to the top of the Mount of Olives, an ambitious Arab boy meets us along the path, dragging a tattered burro by a rope. "You ride? Yes?" he asks. "Only three shekels."

We all laugh, thinking of Jesus' triumphal ride into Jerusalem on a donkey. In fact, we are nearly to the village of Bethsaida where Jesus borrowed His animal. I feel certain that the donkey He rode wasn't as small and mangy as this one—nor was there a price tag attached. This squat, swaybacked burro doesn't look like it could carry the boy up the steep hill, let alone an adult. But our guide convinces a weary, white-haired woman in our group to accept a ride. They haggle the price down to one shekel, and we help the woman climb on. Away she goes, riding sidesaddle, laughing like a schoolgirl, her feet dangling inches from the dirt.

As we continue our ascent, our guide decides to teach us a song from Psalm 122, one of the Songs of Ascents (Psalms 120–134). "I rejoiced with those who said to me, 'Let us go to the house of the Lord'" (v. 1). He explains that Jewish travelers would sing psalms like this one as they made their way to Jerusalem for each of the three yearly pilgrimage festivals. Over time, the words would become as familiar to them as our beloved Christmas carols, sung year after year in celebration. And so we reach the crest of the mountain singing—and panting—and pause to rest.

The view from the summit steals what little breath I have left. The Temple Mount and the Old City of Jerusalem glimmer in the distance, their golden limestone walls and buildings gilded with morning sunlight. Except for the dome of the Muslim shrine that now stands where the Temple once did, this might have been the same view that Jesus and countless other Passover pilgrims saw two thousand years ago. Joy and excitement flood through me as I gaze at the beautiful panorama. The excitement in Jesus' day must have been electrifying when, after three years of speculation and controversy, He finally allowed His followers to publicly proclaim that He was the long-awaited Messiah, riding on a donkey.

The crowds cheered and burst into joyous song. They might have been singing the traditional Passover hymns as they climbed this hill, and now the words seem stunningly appropriate: "With boughs in hand, join in the festal procession . . . O Lord, save us (Hosanna!) . . . Blessed is he who comes in the name of the Lord" (Psalm 118:25–27). The people had sung this psalm all their lives, and now the words and images sprang to life before their eyes in Jesus' triumphal procession. No wonder their shouts reached across the valley to Jerusalem. To get a taste of their ecstasy, imagine standing in church on Christmas morning singing "Joy to the World, the Lord is come! Let earth receive her king!"—and suddenly, Jesus returns! Our long-awaited Savior and King stands right in front of us! All of the songs we've sung and the Scriptures we've read that spoke of His second coming are fulfilled before us.

That's what happened in Jerusalem that day. The ecstatic crowds who greeted their Messiah expected a political leader, and this was His coronation. They waved palm branches, symbols of victory, high in the air the way we wave the flag in a Fourth of July parade. Others shrugged off their cloaks and spread them on the ground to line His path. I have a hall closet filled with jackets and coats, so it wouldn't cost me much to lay one of them on the ground beneath the donkey's muddy, trampling feet. But to the people in Jesus' day, their outer robe may have been the only one they owned, an all-purpose garment that served as a coat during the day, a blanket at night, a pouch for carrying groceries or babies, and much, much more. To spread it at Jesus' feet was a costly sacrifice. But what better way to pledge loyalty to their long-awaited king? Scripture was being fulfilled! "Rejoice greatly, O Daughter of Zion! Shout, Daughter of Jerusalem! See, your king comes to you, righteous and having salvation, gentle and riding on a donkey" (Zechariah 9:9).

The day that we celebrate as Palm Sunday was also an important date on the Jewish religious calendar. It was the day that each family chose the lamb—a male without blemish—that they would sacrifice for the Passover feast in a few days (Exodus 12:3). The crowd might have thought they were choosing a king who would bring freedom from the hated Romans, but instead they were choosing their Passover Lamb who would bring a much greater and more lasting liberation.

I long to sing another psalm as we finish resting and start hiking downhill, but the eastern slope of the Mount of Olives looks very different today than it did in Jesus' day. Our journey takes us through a Jewish cemetery, past thousands and thousands of whitewashed graves. Black-clothed mourners gather around one of them for a funeral, so we proceed in respectful silence. Many of the grave markers have piles of small stones on them left by mourners, reminding me of another episode in the story of Jesus' triumphal entry.

"Teacher, rebuke your disciples!" the unbelieving Pharisees bellowed above the singing and shouting. They recognized the dangerous political implications of the palm-waving celebration, and knew that the Romans would, too. Jesus refused. "If they keep quiet, the stones will cry out," He replied (Luke 19:39, 40).

Israel has the rockiest terrain I have ever seen, so the shouts from millions of cheering stones would have been deafening. But the Pharisees, who knew the Scriptures by heart, would have recognized Jesus' reply as a quote from the prophet Habakkuk. Instead of rebuking His followers, Jesus was rebuking them! "Woe to him who builds his realm by unjust gain to set his nest on high . . . The stones of the wall will cry out" (2:9, 11). Habakkuk warns of God's judgment against corruption and bloodshed, and ends with a magnificent Messianic prophesy: "For the earth will be filled with the knowledge of the glory of the Lord, as the waters cover the sea" (v. 14). Jesus was telling the Pharisees that God would soon judge them. But the joyful, cheering celebration that began on Palm Sunday could never be stopped.

We find more enterprising Arab boys waiting for us at the bottom of the hill, hawking blurry postcards and flimsy souvenirs. "One shekel! One shekel!" they call out. Our bus is also waiting. It's too difficult to walk to the Temple Mount from here and cross the modern highway that zooms through the Kidron Valley. Besides, the Golden Gate that Jesus would have entered to reach the Temple is sealed shut. But I look back at the Mount of Olives as we drive away, still picturing that Palm Sunday and imagining the wonder and joy that must have overwhelmed the disciples.

Jesus had explained to His followers what would happen to Him when they reached Jerusalem, but I don't think they really believed Him. I'm sure that Peter, James, John, and the others still clung to the hope that the Messiah would be a political king who would sit on David's throne and govern Israel. The Palm Sunday victory parade and the masses of people pledging their allegiance to Him probably buoyed those hopes. And memories of that celebration probably added to their despair and confusion when the king they had chosen turned out to be a lamb who was sacrificed on Passover.

I have publicly proclaimed Jesus as my Messiah and Lord, but like the Palm Sunday revelers, I wonder if I'm also guilty of creating false expectations of who Jesus is and what He wants to do in my life. I have prayed for salvation from painful circumstances as if expecting Him to make all my troubles march away like retreating Roman soldiers. When they don't, I'm disappointed and discouraged. But maybe, instead of changing my circumstances, Jesus wants to use those circumstances to change me. Isn't that what His sacrifice on Calvary was really about? To set me free from my sins so that I could become more like Him?

Before I toss my coat in His path in a giddy Palm Sunday parade, swept along with the crowd, perhaps I need to examine more carefully what Jesus really meant when He said, "In this world you will have trouble. But take heart! I have overcome the world" (John 16:33).

The Last Supper

The room bears no resemblance to the one in the DaVinci painting. We have climbed a steep, narrow set of stairs to an upper room, arranged as it might have looked for the Last Supper. The shadowy space has few windows, the plain stone walls are unadorned. Lit only by oil lamps, it seems more like evening in here than daytime. A long, low table fills the center of the room, surrounded by rugs and mats. We gather around it, reclining on the floor with our elbows propped on the table—something my mother would chide me for doing, but it's the only way to eat comfortably.

In Jesus' day, this table would have held all the traditional items for the Passover meal: bitter herbs and salt water to remind them of tears and slavery; a gooey concoction called *charoset* to symbolize their labor with bricks and mortar; unleavened bread to remember their hasty departure; and roasted lamb to recall the blood of salvation on their doorposts. Jesus and the disciples had celebrated Passover since childhood, eating the same foods, singing the traditional songs, reading the well-loved Scriptures, and so every feature of this meal was familiar to them. "I have eagerly desired to eat this Passover with you before I suffer," Jesus began. "For I tell you, I will not eat it again until it finds fulfillment in the kingdom of God" (Luke 22:15–16). He was about to teach the disciples His final lessons, so they must be important ones.

Once our group has gathered around the table, our guide has a surprise for us. "We are going to wash each other's feet," he says. I stifle a groan. I don't want to bare my feet in public, much less have someone near enough to smell them. I've been hiking all morning in sweaty shoes—and hiking for a week in the desert before that in the same pair. I'll sit back and watch, thank you.

I'm not the only one who balks. The ritual exposes our stubborn American individualism. We don't want anyone to serve us so intimately, glimpsing our ugly blisters and the dirt we keep carefully hidden. Nor do we like to see other people's warts and calluses. Kindly keep your imperfections and wounds hidden from view.

If I'm reacting with obstinate pride and uneasiness, how must the disciples have felt when Jesus announced that He was going to wash their feet? Imagine their disbelief when He removed His robe and dressed as a servant to do the menial job of hauling water upstairs, then kneeling to perform a slave's task. The disciples walked on dusty, manure-strewn roads all day. None of them had Odor-Eaters in their sandals. None of them had gone for a pedicure beforehand. Peter folded his arms and shook his head in defiance. "No. You shall never wash my feet" (John 13:8). He had the nerve to say *no* to Jesus?

Was I just as guilty?

Seeing myself in Peter's reaction, I have a change of heart. I submit to the ritual, knowing there might be an important lesson to learn.

"Partner with a stranger," the guide tells us, "not a family member or friend." I kneel down in front of a woman I barely know and remove her shoes, then bathe her feet in the basin of water. When I finish, she washes mine. It is very humbling to kneel and serve, even more humbling to be served. Yet this was precisely the point that Jesus was trying to make. We need to be vulnerable and honest with each other—and with Him. He knows all of our warts anyway, so why not bring them into the light and let Him wash us clean? And the hands that He uses to do it are those of my fellow Christians, His body.

"Do you understand what I have done for you?" Jesus asked when He was finished. "Now that I, your Lord and Teacher, have washed your feet, you also should wash one another's feet" (John 13:12, 14). Disciples are supposed to watch the Master and imitate His actions, not merely parrot His words. If He humbled himself in the role of a servant, then I need to, as well. And if He tells me to take off my shoes and stop hiding the dirt and ugliness so that my church family can help me get clean, do I dare fold my arms and shake my head in defiance?

It occurs to me that Jesus must have washed Judas' feet. I recall a time when I felt wounded and betrayed by the words and actions of another Christian, but if I want to follow Jesus' example, my response should be to show her grace. To not only forgive her but to serve her. I can do neither on my own, only with His help.

As we take our places at the table again, Jesus' concluding words prick my heart: "Now that you know these things, you will be blessed if you do them" (John 13:17).

And I will miss out on a great blessing if I don't.

Communion

A real Passover meal is an extended celebration, beginning at sundown and lasting late into the night. We can't recapture its depth in a mere hour, but our guide shares some of the highlights with us. For Jesus and His fellow Jews, the meal commemorated their covenant with God and rescue from slavery in Egypt. But as Jesus celebrated it with His disciples on the night before His crucifixion, He transformed the traditional Passover wine and bread into our commemorative meal, celebrating His new covenant and our rescue from slavery to sin. Each time we partake of His body and blood, we're affirming that we are His disciples, that we will do whatever the Lord tells us to do instead of following our own stubborn desires.

If we were eating a full Passover meal here in this room, we would drink four cups of wine throughout the course of the evening. Each cup represents one of the four promises God made to Israel on that first Passover night in Egypt (Exodus 6:6). The first is, "I will bring you out from under the yoke of the Egyptians." The second, "I will free you from being slaves to them." And the third is the one I believe Jesus drank when He said, "This cup is the new covenant in my blood, which is poured out for you" (Luke 22:20). It represents the promise, "I will redeem you with an outstretched arm" (Exodus 6:6). When His Passover meal ended a few hours later, His redemption would begin.

There remained a fourth cup of wine, but Jesus said, "I will not drink again of the fruit of the vine until the kingdom of God comes" (Luke 22:18). He drank that final cup as He took a sip of wine while suffering on the cross, fulfilling the

Grapevine

final promise, "I will take you as my own people" (Exodus 6:7). Then He announced, "It is finished" (John 19:30).

As the guide continues to explain the Passover traditions, I silently marvel at how thoroughly God has embedded the story of Christ's salvation into these rituals: How three portions of unleavened bread are placed in a special cloth called The Unity; how the middle piece is removed and broken in two, then hidden for a time; how it is later redeemed with silver and broken by the host into bite-sized pieces that are shared around the table. "This is my body given for you" (Luke 22:19).

No one who celebrated this meal year after year could have missed this rich symbolism, especially when Christ enacted Passover before their eyes, dying on the cross at the very hour that the nation's Passover lamb was being sacrificed at the Temple. And yet the disciples did miss it, at first. They had created their own images of what the Messiah would be like and what He would do, and when His gruesome death shattered those images, their lives seemed to shatter, as well. But how infinitely better His salvation is than the one their limited minds had envisioned.

I, too, have created images of what my life should be like and how God should answer my prayers. I confess that when I hold those broken dreams in my hands, I feel angry with God. And yet His answers to my prayers have always turned out to be better in the end than what I could have planned. Always. Even when the answer was no.

The traditional Passover meal ends with singing and prayer. We have Jesus' closing prayer recorded for us in John 17. Surprisingly, He prayed for His disciples and us that night. He prayed for our protection and blessing and fellowship:

"May they be brought to complete unity to let the world know that you sent me" (v. 23).

The Passover Feast ended. "When they had sung a hymn, they went out to the Mount of Olives" (Mark 14:26). Before that day would end at sundown on Friday, one of His disciples would betray Him. The rest would scatter in fear. Peter would deny three times that he even knew Jesus, much less was His disciple. Jesus would die on a cross.

I sit uncomfortably at the low table, unaccustomed to the hard floor and the even harder lessons. In a room much like this one, on a night that celebrated freedom and God's miraculous deliverance, Jesus taught what it means to truly be His disciple. We are to serve one another—and that means swallowing my pride and self-sufficiency and allowing my church family to see my hurts and doubts and fears. We are to trust His plans when we pray instead of dictating how we want Him to act. And we are to be one in mind and heart as a witness to an unbelieving world.

Judas ate the covenant meal. He called himself a disciple and allowed Jesus to wash his feet. He even kissed Him in greeting as a faithful disciple would. But his actions betrayed his words. The other disciples also promised to follow Him, but when the crucial moment arrived, they scattered and denied knowing Him. At Communion, I also drink the cup of the new covenant and call Him Lord, but do my actions betray Him or disown Him?

We leave the shadowy room and file down the stairs, emerging into the sunlight. My feet may be clean, but I feel painfully exposed. It seems much too easy to glibly call myself His disciple—and more difficult than I realized to live up to that name.

Gethsemane

When Jesus's Passover meal with His disciples ended late that night, He walked with them down the hillside from the Upper Room and across Jerusalem in the dark. As they passed other houses along the way, they probably heard laughter and singing spilling from the open windows as Jews all over the city celebrated with their families. Outside the city walls, He crossed the narrow Kidron Valley to the Garden of Gethsemane on the lower slopes of the Mount of Olives.

A large church dominates the traditional place of Jesus' agonized prayer on the night before His crucifixion, but our tour guide leads us to a private olive grove behind the church. An Israeli gardener, pruning shears in hand, opens the gate to the walled enclosure for our group, then closes it behind us, muffling the noise and rush of modern Jerusalem. It's easy to imagine that the garden where Jesus prayed was peaceful, too, as the hushed city and His hapless disciples slept. Their sleepiness is understandable. They have just eaten an enormous meal and have drunk the four required cups of wine in a celebration that rarely ends before midnight. I would be drowsy, too.

Olive trees have flourished for centuries on this western slope of the Mount of Olives, as they do to this day. The ancient trees are not very tall, about the height of an apple tree, but the gnarled trunks of some of the oldest ones are as big around as a barrel. There is no fruit on the branches this winter day since olives are harvested in the fall, but the trees' slender silvery-green leaves remain on the branches year-round.

Directly across the narrow Kidron Valley from us is the mountain where God's Temple once stood. If Jesus had looked up from His prayers, He might have seen the Temple's golden roof glowing softly in the moonlight. Jews from all over the known world gathered there to worship and to watch the priests sacrifice lambs every morning and evening. Since the altar fire burned continuously throughout the night, Jesus might have smelled the aroma of the evening sacrifice as He prayed.

Our guide explains that Gethsemane means "oil press"; Christ prayed in the Garden of the Oil Press. Old Testament worship required large quantities of olive oil to accompany the sacrifices and to burn continuously in the sanctuary's golden lamps. To extract the valuable oil, the olives were first bruised and crushed, then squeezed and pressed beneath heavy stone weights. Our guide picks up a discarded olive from beneath one of the trees and crushes it in his hand. The first juice that oozes out is the reddish-brown color of blood.

On the night that Jesus prayed here, He was about to be broken and crushed, then placed beneath the tremendous weight of our sins. His sweat was as great drops of blood as He prayed beneath the rustling branches of the olive trees, "Father, if you are willing, take this cup from me; yet not my will, but yours be done" (Luke 22:42). After reading this Scripture passage to us, our guide invites us to find a quiet place alone in the garden to pray. We scatter, and I find a large rock to sit on.

While our guide was reading Scripture to us, I was watching the gardener quietly going about his work, pruning the trees in his care. But he wasn't simply removing a dead twig or two, snipping gently here and there. This man has been chopping ruthlessly. As I've watched him mutilate these poor trees, I've been tempted to stand up and shout, "Stop! That's too much! You're going to kill them!"

Admittedly, I know little about gardening. When I prune the greenery in my yard back home, I'm much too compassionate, fearful of damaging an expensive tree or shrub. Perhaps that's why the crab apple tree outside my office window looks tangled and overgrown, and why my lilac bush hasn't bloomed in years. Even so, this gardener was going too far in my opinion, chopping as if he had a grudge against the trees. The pile of discarded branches accumulating on the ground looked larger than the volume of branches that remained on the stumps. Maybe he intended to pull up the stumps when he finished, then raze the grove and plant a different crop. But no, this was a typical winter's pruning, our guide assured me when I asked him.

An hour or so before Jesus prayed here on the night of His arrest, He had shared the Passover Feast with His disciples. The lengthy meal gave Him an opportunity to teach His final lessons—the last cramming session before the big exam when they'd be left on their own. One of those lessons was "I am the true vine, and my Father is the gardener. He cuts off every branch in me that bears no fruit, while every branch that does bear fruit he prunes so that it will be even more fruitful" (John 15:1–2). As I watched, this Israeli gardener demonstrated Jesus' lesson. True, the dead, fruitless branches deserved to be cut off. But he also pruned the healthy, fruit-bearing branches so they would bear even more fruit—assuming that the trees lived through this massacre, I thought to myself.

So often in this past year, I have questioned God as I faced losses and changes that seemed to cut too deeply. Even some of the fruit-bearing branches in my life had been ruthlessly chopped off. I have felt as wounded and mutilated as these truncated trees as I lost parts of myself. "Stop!" I have wanted to shout. "You're cutting too much! I'll have nothing left!" But now I see that God, like this gardener, knows what He is doing. These olive trees will bear even more fruit next season. And so, in faith, will I.

The gardener stoops to gather the fallen branches and carry them away to be burned. I know that if I returned to this grove next fall, the harvest of olives would weigh down the remaining branches. This isn't the first season that the gardener has radically pruned these trees, and it certainly won't be the last. The cycle is meant to continue, season after season: pruning, growing, bearing fruit, producing oil, pruning once again. "This is to my Father's glory, that you bear much fruit, showing yourselves to be my disciples" (John 15:8).

The stripping away that God does in our lives only looks harsh to our untrained eyes. He asks us to bear it patiently, for our own good, trusting that abundant fruit will follow to His glory. May my prayer be, "Not my will, but yours be done."

The High Priest's House

The view from the High Priest's house is stunning. Caiaphas had the wealth and power and influence to situate his home on one of the city's many hills where he could survey the surrounding mountains and valleys. The creamy limestone of God's Holy Temple would have glowed in the distance, its golden roof gleaming in the sunlight. We have traveled here from the Garden of Gethsemane by bus, but after His arrest, Jesus would have been forced to walk all this way in the dark of night, bound and shackled and prodded forward by bullying Temple guards. His faithful disciples had scattered and run.

Of course a church now occupies this site, but the long set of stone steps leading up the hill from street level dates from the first century. I can walk where Jesus walked with certainty—if indeed I want to arrive at the place of His unjust trial, hear the false accusations hurled at Him, witness the unfair verdict of "guilty and deserving of death."

Inside the church, we descend another set of stone steps leading down to a dank, cold dungeon, carved into the bedrock beneath Caiaphas' house. Iron rings imbedded in stone walls once shackled the prisoners to prevent escape. Again, I am aware of the authenticity of this place. I am following in Jesus' footsteps as He sat imprisoned here, awaiting trial before the Sanhedrin. Without warning, our guide extinguishes the lights, leaving us in darkness. Jesus, the light of the world, sat in this darkness, chained and beaten. For me.

I am glad to return outside to the courtyard, but my relief lasts only a moment. This is where Peter, once a faithful disciple, denied three times that he ever knew Jesus, swearing an oath. As he huddled around the fire with the others to escape the dark, uncertain night, he had no idea how this crisis in his life would end. All he could see was that the man he had followed and trusted as his Messiah now sat in a dungeon. The religious movement he had believed in and sacrificed his career for had come to nothing, and there was a very good chance that Peter would also face arrest. Jesus had said that He would be betrayed, that He would suffer and die, then rise again on the third day. But promises have a way of vanishing like smoke, driven by the strong winds of fear when we're facing trouble and uncertainty. Peter must have forgotten Isaiah's prophecy, "The earth will be full of the knowledge of the Lord as the waters cover the sea" (Isaiah 11:9).

Like Peter, I have uttered words of betrayal as my fear shouted louder than my faith, saying in effect, "I don't know Jesus!" As darkness extinguished the light of His word, I've doubted that His promises would ever come true for me. I may not have screamed my denials in a public courtyard, but whenever I give in to fear and worry, my soul denies Christ's power and promises. Yes, I understand how Peter felt when he stood here that night.

I hear singing in the distance, and a moment later, a tour group from Africa emerges through the church doors wearing colorful *dashikis* and turbans. They are singing, clapping, praising God, and though I don't understand their language, I recognize praise and joy and the name *Jesu*. Could Peter have imagined on that dark, hopeless night that one day the praises of his African brothers and sisters would fill this courtyard? I don't think so. Our imaginations are too limited, our faith too small. But here they are, men and women of God just like Peter, disciples of Jesus from a distant continent.

One of Christ's last promises to Peter—and to us—was "Surely I am with you always, to the very end of the age" (Matthew 28:20). When the only thing I can see is a dark night and a shadowy courtyard, when fear begins whispering words of betrayal, I can hang on to Christ's promise. With Him, things are never as they seem.

Calvary

Our journey through Passion Week continues as we wind our way through the narrow streets of Jerusalem's Old City. The *Via Dolorosa*, or Walk of Sorrow, is marked out for us, showing the route that Jesus walked to the cross. It's hard for me to think about what that final journey may have been like as I maneuver to avoid the crush of people and vehicles. Scripture says the chief priests first forced Jesus to climb up the Temple mount to the Antonia Fortress at dawn and stand before Pilate. By 9:00 a.m., He had been cruelly flogged and mocked and beaten and led outside the walls to be cruci-fied. At the time when He was being nailed to the cross, the Temple priests were sacrificing the morning Passover lamb for the sins of the people. As His lifeless body was being taken down before sunset that day, the priests would be offering the evening Passover sacrifice at the Temple.

And so we come to Calvary. According to traditions that are thousands of years old, both the hill where Jesus was crucified and the garden tomb where He lay until His resurrection are housed within the walls of the Church of the Holy Sepulcher. The site was outside the city walls in Jesus' day but is now within the walls of the Old City, near the Arab bazaar. The shapeless, windowless church appears very unpromising from the outside with its stained, mismatched stones, not at all like the soaring cathedrals I've seen in Europe. Its antiquity and the fact that men have fought over this church for centuries are probably to blame for its appearance, causing the fortress-like buildings to be built and razed, won and lost numerous times.

We walk into the church through an arched doorway and enter an altogether different world. These holy places have been gilded and polished and adorned by thousands of years of Christian devotion until I feel as though I can hardly move forward through the glittering clutter. The trappings of or-nate religion seem to weigh me down: gleaming silver and bronze, embroidered tapestries, sputtering candles, cloying incense, priests in flowing robes, marble statues. To say that it no longer resembles a place of execution or a graveyard is an understatement.

I wait in line to climb a short set of steps to where the cross supposedly stood, but once there, I can't see past the gaudiness to imagine Christ's passion. A man in a brown robe prods me and my fellow tourists to keep moving. I wait in line again to peer inside a square, stone monument, all that remains of the rocky hillside from which the borrowed tomb was hewn. Empty or not, it no longer resembles a tomb. I have to confess that since I don't belong to the religious traditions represented in this church, I find it difficult to feel awe or amazement or any of the other emotions that I thought I would.

Our guide, a Jewish believer in Christ, agrees that it's difficult to envision how Calvary and the empty tomb may have looked by touring this church. He offers to take us to a place where we can more easily picture what it may have looked like two thousand years ago. And so we leave and walk through the Old City's claustrophobic streets again to the crowded Arab market. Within moments, we are jammed together with black-draped Muslim women and souvenir-sellers hawking their wares. The shopkeepers' aggressive shouts sound angry: "Look! Buy! Buy! One shekel!"

"Keep walking. Don't stop," our guide says.

We've all been warned to be on guard against pickpockets, so I quicken my steps until at last we leave the Old City through the Damascus Gate. We are now in the Muslim section of modern Jerusalem, and though the streets are wider, they still overflow with people and traffic, shouting street vendors, and honking buses, all in a hurry. I want to escape the noise and congestion, but our guide halts us on a busy street corner.

"Here!" he says, gesturing to the hubbub all around us. "Here, in a very public place like this, outside the walls—this is where the Romans would crucify Christ. They would make a public spectacle of the condemned men, lifting them up to shame and ridicule in front of everyone passing by." During a crowded pilgrimage festival like Passover the streets would have resembled Times Square on New Year's Eve.

I can't bear to think of Christ nailed to a cross on a street like this, naked and vulnerable, suffering and dying as people hurried past, uncaring, unconcerned, stopping only to mock Him. The words "He bore our shame" take on new meaning for me. I bow my head, feeling unworthy, overwhelmed by the love that compelled Him to die.

We continue to walk for another block or two up a small hill until we reach the entrance to a walled garden. This peaceful, tree-filled grove contains a first-century tomb in its original state and I find it much easier to visualize the biblical events here. Whether or not this is the authentic site doesn't matter.

We walk to the rear of the garden to view the craggy, undeveloped cliff that is part of this hill and see that the weathered rocks bear the features of a skull. As we make our way to a secluded grove to celebrate Communion, I hear voices and singing. Groups of tourists from all over the world sit tucked in private grottos, celebrating Communion, as well. Their songs are in several languages—German, Korean, Italian, and others that I can't identify. Some of the tunes are familiar even if the language isn't, but I don't need an interpreter to understand what is being said: "This is my body, broken for you; My blood, shed for you." I sit in the private garden reserved for our group and can't stop my tears as I partake of Christ's body and blood, surrounded by the colorful babble of praise.

Afterward, we come at last to the unadorned tomb, dating from the time of Christ. It resembles a rugged cave, carved into the natural, rocky hillside. Beside the mouth of the tomb stands an enormous flat stone disc that can be rolled in front of the opening to seal it. The stone has been rolled away. The tomb is empty. This is what the women who came to the garden early that first Easter morning, the last day of the Passover festival, would have seen. The huge, round stone that once sealed the entrance had been rolled away. The narrow stone ledge inside held only the discarded grave cloths.

Passover consists of three separate feasts: the Feast of Passover, the Feast of Unleavened Bread, and the Feast of Firstfruits. Since Jewish days are reckoned from sundown to sundown, Jesus ate the traditional Passover meal with His disciples, then was arrested, condemned, and crucified, all on the Feast of Passover. As soon as the sun set, another day and the second feast began, the Feast of Unleavened Bread. Jesus was laid in the tomb at the start of that feast and the tomb's opening was sealed shut with a heavy stone.

During this second feast, worshipers wave sheaves of wheat as they thank God for the gift of bread from the earth. They remember the manna that He provided in the wilderness, "bread" that was free and sufficient, satisfying all of their needs as they gathered it in faith. "I am the bread of life," Jesus said. "I tell you the truth, unless a kernel of wheat falls to the ground and dies, it remains only a single seed. But if it dies, it produces many seeds" (John 12:24). I doubt if His disciples or His mother or any of the others would have re-called those words as they watched Him being buried in the tomb as the Feast of Unleavened Bread began.

It so happened that the Sabbath day also began at sundown on that Good Friday, and so instead of anointing Jesus' body or mourning at His grave, His Jewish followers were required to return to their homes and rest from their labors. I imagine them huddling together, grieving, unable to do any work such as lighting a fire or cooking food or walking more than a very short distance. I imagine them waiting, feeling helpless. As helpless as I am to save myself. As helpless as I am to do anything to take away my own sins and reconnect with God. For the disciples, that long Sabbath must have been a day of sorrow and disaster. Once a kernel of wheat is buried underground it is invisible, and so they were unable to see—or imagine—the great harvest that God would soon bring. But as I look inside the empty tomb here in this garden and then emerge again into the sunlight, I am surrounded by evidence of that harvest as Christians from all over the world praise God in dozens of languages and share the body and blood of Christ.

That first Easter Sunday two thousand years ago happened to fall on the third feast day of the Passover festival, the Feast of Firstfruits. On this day, worshipers brought the very first sheaves of grain from their fields and offered them as sacrifices to God. The full harvest was still weeks away, but they would give God the first and best of their grain in faith, trusting that He would provide more. The Feast of Firstfruits is always celebrated on a Sunday, regardless of which day Passover and Unleavened Bread happen to fall. Since Passover is decided by the phases of the moon, the three feasts rarely occur on three consecutive days. But in God's perfect timing, in the year that Christ was crucified, they did. Such precision helps me trust His timing in my own life. This was a sign of God's providence, the sign of Jonah: "For as Jonah was three days and three nights in the belly of a huge fish, so the Son of Man will be three days and three nights in the heart of the earth" (Matthew 12:40).

The fact that Jesus was raised to life on the Feast of Firstfruits is God's promise to us that we'll also share in His resurrection. The apostle Paul saw the significance when he wrote: "For as in Adam all die, so in Christ all will be made alive. But each in his own turn: Christ, the firstfruits; then, when he comes, those who belong to him" (1 Corinthians 15:22–23). This decaying world around me isn't all that there is. Christ promised a new heaven and a new earth where our resurrected bodies will never suffer pain or sorrow or death. But for now, I live in this world as His new creation. "We were therefore buried with him through baptism into death in order that, just as Christ was raised from the dead through the glory of the Father, we too may live a new life" (Romans 6:4).

I'm reluctant to leave the garden and reenter the world, but that's exactly what we are supposed to do. "Don't cling to me," Jesus told the women that Easter Sunday. "Go and tell the others" (see John 20:17). The minute I step outside the garden walls and see cars and buses and people streaming by, I am hurled back from the past and into the present. I'm standing smack-dab in the middle of the Muslim section of Jerusalem, confronted with the realization that these hurrying, rushing people don't know Christ. They don't know His love, His forgiveness. The truth hits me hard.

An hour ago, before I envisioned Jesus hanging in shame on a street like this, before I partook of His body and blood, before I walked into the sunlight after viewing the dark, empty tomb, I saw these people and thought of pickpockets and terrorists, strangers from a foreign culture who practice a foreign religion. Now, if only for a brief moment, I see them as God does. They are dearly loved. Loved so much that Christ suffered and bled and died for them.

If only they knew.

I doubt that they'll discover the truth by visiting the Church of the Holy Sepulcher and watching the Christian tourists and listening to the chanted rituals. I doubt if they would grasp it even after a visit to the garden tomb.

If only they knew.

If only I loved as He does. If only there was less of me and more of Christ.

For God so loved the world that he gave his one and only Son, that whoever believes in him shall not perish but have eternal life. For God did not send his Son into the world to condemn the world, but to save the world through him.

John 3:16–17

A New Prayer for the Journey

My loving Savior and Lord,

I remember the Walk of Sorrows that You walked for me, and I praise You for Your unfathomable love. You created the universe in love, created us for loving fellowship with You, and then demonstrated Your love at Calvary. I confess that I feel unworthy of it. Jesus, the punishment You faced should have been mine—punishment for my pride, for choosing my own will instead of Yours, for failing to love others as You love them. Thank You for taking my place. Thank You for Your glorious resurrection and the promise that we will share in it one day. Thank You for the new brothers and sisters You have given me from every tribe and nation and language. Forgive me for denying Your power and goodness every time I give in to worry and fear; for forgetting that as high as the heavens are above the earth, so are Your ways above mine. I pray for the faith to offer up my plans, my will, to Yours. Help me to submit to Your pruning in my life so that I will bear fruit for Your glory. May my best prayer always be, "Not my will but Thine be done."

   Amen

8

THE JUDEAN
COUNTRYSIDE

Sing to the Lord, praise his name; proclaim his salvation day
after day. Declare his glory among the nations, his marvelous
deeds among all peoples.

Psalm 96:2–3

When I've read of people in Scripture walking from town to town, I never imagined how much territory they went through or how hilly the terrain was. I have a newfound respect for their physical fitness! On our journey from Jerusalem to the Mediterranean coast, we're traveling through the region known as Judea in Jesus' day. The hills are green with trees and crops, dotted with rocks and villages. In between the hills, the open country flourishes with orchards and vineyards.

We leave the main highway to stop at the fortress of Latrun, a genuine military fort used as recently as the Six-Day War in 1967. Its limestone walls bear wounds from cannonballs, artillery, and machine-gun fire. I should be used to climbing Israel's many hills by now, but I'm still breathless when I reach the fort from the parking lot. The view is worth it, though. The main road from the coastal plain to Jerusalem stretches below us in clear view, making Israel's approaching enemies clearly visible, too. Like a game of "king of the hill," the imposing stone structure stands ready, hands on hips, as if daring someone to attack.

The broad green Valley of Aijalon lies below me, sprinkled with fields and vineyards and wrapped in the surrounding mountains' embrace. I am continually surprised by Israel's diverse beauty—and history. This is the famous valley where God caused the sun to stand still in the middle of the day so Joshua could defeat his enemies. "There has never been a day like it before or since, a day when the Lord listened to a man. Surely the Lord was fighting for Israel!" (Joshua 10:14).

Today the Fortress of Latrun is the site of a war memorial for the Israeli Defense Forces, a place where families and fellow soldiers come to honor loved ones who died in battle. The broad plaza surrounding the fort serves as an outdoor tank museum with more than one hundred armored vehicles of various makes and models on display. Our guide's descriptions of their firepower fascinate the men in our tour group, but I grow bored. I turn to gaze at the view of the Valley of Aijalon. The sun sits low in the winter sky, but I try to imagine it rising to its zenith—and then staying there for a full day. That's what the Bible says happened as Israel battled her enemies here, laying claim to the Promised Land. But a few weeks earlier, Joshua, the commander-in-chief of Israel's army, had made a terrible mistake.

After resounding victories at Jericho and at Ai, Joshua met with a delegation of foreigners who came to him seeking a peace treaty. He knew that God had forbidden him to make treaties with the people of the land but these men persisted. "We have come from a distant country," they said. "We aren't your enemies." They looked bedraggled and road-weary, their bread dry and moldy, their sandals worn out, as if they had journeyed many miles. Joshua believed their sad story and without praying or consulting God, he signed a peace treaty with them, swearing an oath before God to be their allies. Surprise! It had all been a trick—the moldy bread, the secondhand shoes. The men hadn't traveled far at all, only from Gibeon, one of the Canaanite cities slated for destruction. Joshua had foolishly compromised with the enemy and now he was stuck with a treaty God had forbidden him to make.

I love this glimpse of a Bible hero as human and fallible. Born in Egypt, Joshua had seen the ten plagues in person, experienced God's miraculous rescue from the angel of death, walked through the Red Sea with walls of water towering on each side of him. He had followed the pillar of fire through the wilderness, eaten manna, and sipped water from the rock. Joshua had remained faithful when nearly everyone else in his generation had failed, and he was one of only two spies who believed God and gave a good report about the Promised Land. At every opportunity to give in to fear or to complain or to worship false gods, Joshua had chosen to trust God again and again. He was one of only a handful of people still alive who had journeyed with God all the way from Egypt, and God had chosen him to take Moses' place after his death.

And now Joshua had made a terrible mistake. He had compromised with the enemy. Did he feel like kicking himself? Did he go into his tent and weep with frustration over his failure? Frankly, I think he did. Joshua is not a flat storybook character but a flesh-and-blood person, like me. And he must have felt certain that God was all finished with him.

Before Joshua could write his letter of resignation, a messenger arrived from Gibeon—the city he had just made his foolish alliance with. The kings of five powerful city-states had formed a coalition and were marching toward Gibeon to attack it. The people of Gibeon pleaded with Joshua for help, begging him to honor the treaty and save them. Joshua, whose name means "The Lord saves," must have wondered if he had forfeited the right to save anyone. But God said, "Do not be afraid of them; I have given them into your hand. Not one of them will be able to withstand you" (Joshua 10:8).

There it is: God's grace, mercy, and forgiveness, even in the Old Testament. Joshua could pick himself up and go forward after he'd failed—and so can we. Joshua mustered Israel's army and marched to the rescue.

The city of Gibeon is in Israel's central highlands, and getting there from where Joshua was camped required an uphill journey of more than fifteen miles. The road back after we've disobeyed always seems uphill, doesn't it? Maybe the strenuous effort will remind us not to repeat our mistake. Joshua's rescue at Gibeon succeeded, and the five invading armies retreated down the Valley of Aijalon. But Joshua wanted a thorough victory. This time he would do it right and destroy every last enemy. No more compromises. But he was running out of daylight—and so he prayed.

In response, the heavens unleashed an arsenal of hailstones, God's cannonballs, striking down the enemy as they ran.

Then a miracle: The sun stood still! It continued to shine until every last enemy was hunted down and destroyed.

As the tide of battle began to turn, the five enemy kings hid inside a cave. "Roll boulders in front of the entrance," Joshua told his men, "so they can't escape. We'll deal with them after the battle is finished" (see Joshua 10:18–19). When that time came, he ordered his commanders to stand with their feet on the defeated kings' necks. "This is what the Lord will do to all the enemies you are going to fight," he told them (Joshua 10:25). The bodies of the slain kings were hung on a tree, a sign designated by God to show that they are under His curse (Deuteronomy 21:22–23).

Before we gave our lives to Christ, the Bible says that we were enemies of God like these Canaanites, following the false gods of our culture, living by our own rules. Because of our sin, we were under a death sentence like they were, like all of disobedient mankind is. But "Christ redeemed us from the curse of the law by becoming a curse for us" (Galatians 3:13). "He himself bore our sins in his body on the tree, so that we might die to sins and live for righteousness" (1 Peter 2:24).

The day that Jesus freed us from that curse was one of the darkest days ever recorded. The sun stopped shining from noon until three in the afternoon as Jesus hung on the cross. Darkness represents divine judgment, and as Jesus, "the light of the world," suffered God's curse on the cross, darkness threatened to engulf the world. For a few hours, it seemed as though the darkness was winning. But Jesus overcame the darkness.

He has done more than His part in the war we're fighting, but His orders to us are clear: "Put to death the misdeeds of the body" (Romans 8:13). That means not holding grudges. Not losing my temper or speaking unloving words.

Not coveting. Forgiving others. And it means conquering any fortresses that are still under enemy control. God fights with me and for me, but compromising with sin is not an option. Am I courageous enough to go to war?

God told the Jewish people to fast and pray each year on the Day of Atonement, examining their lives and confessing their sins. Before partaking of Christ's body and blood at Communion we are told, "A man ought to examine himself" (1 Corinthians 11:28). Repentance is so much more than a halfhearted confession. Any parent who has asked a naughty child for an apology knows what a reluctant, sullen "sorry" sounds like. The word *repent* means to do a complete reversal, turning our back on our sins, taking a brand-new road, walking in an entirely new direction—like Joshua did when he turned his back on compromise and began to fight. If we truly repent, God is merciful and will forgive us, just as He forgave Joshua. But my Jewish friends also tell me that if you find yourself confessing the same sin the following year on the Day of Atonement, something is terribly wrong. I try to remember that warning when I prepare for Communion.

We're commanded to consider ourselves dead to sin, not keep it on life-support or make a peace treaty with it. This requires change, a word most of us hate. No matter how we say it: "Do not let sin reign in your mortal body so that you obey its evil desires" or "Do not offer the parts of your body to sin" (Romans 6:12–13), God's instructions to us sound remarkably like His command to Joshua: "Utterly destroy the enemy." I have a long way to go.

God caused the sun to stand still, allowing Joshua to fight, and now He wants to shine His light into all the dark corners of my heart, revealing areas where I have compromised, showing me strongholds that are still under enemy control. If I let His light shine and shine and then shine some more, I can fight until the enemy is thoroughly defeated. Jesus died so that I could have a new life, not a life lived in captivity or compromise.

I can't do this on my own, of course, any more than Joshua could drive out the enemy all by himself or cause the sun to stand still over the Valley of Aijalon. For Joshua—and for me—the only way to achieve victory is through trusting in God. If I supply the motivation, He'll supply the power to get rid of everything that is displeasing to Him, even when it hurts. Even when I fail and face an uphill battle as I try again.

The cross is much more than a piece of jewelry or a wall decoration. It's a war memorial like this one at Latrun, reminding us not only of the victory that Christ has won, but of the enormous cost of that victory. I don't want to surrender any of the territory that Christ died to redeem by returning to my old, sinful ways. Not when the blood that was spilled on the battlefield was His own.

Watchtower

An hour or so outside of Jerusalem, we leave the main highway and drive up a narrow, winding road to a lookout tower with a commanding view of the Judean hill country. The Israelis call this area the *Shephelah*, or foothills, and it's the place where Samson and King David once roamed. According to John 3:22, "Jesus and his disciples went out into the Judean countryside, where he spent some time with them, and baptized."

But when we arrive at the top of the lookout hill, we discover that we aren't alone. A squadron of Israeli soldiers is using this spot for maneuvers. Army vehicles and equipment fill the parking lot. Their waterproof steel containers hold sophisticated technical gear with telescopes and listening devices and the largest pair of binoculars I have ever seen. Young soldiers in spotless green uniforms have set up these instruments on the ridge and quietly peer off into the distance. They concentrate so intently that they don't seem at all distracted by our arrival.

We climb the spiral steps to the top of the lookout tower and gaze at the view, enjoying the peaceful scenery and the warm winter sunshine. Even though I am looking in the same direction as the soldiers, their powerful military technology enables them to see much farther into the distance than I can. Someone from our group asks the commander what his soldiers are doing. His curt reply: "Practicing."

These soldiers are practicing vigilance, and I'm grateful. I have never felt threatened or in danger while visiting Israel because even though the nation is currently at peace, her army remains watchful for any dangers that might disturb that peace. I see the soldiers' disciplined movements, the sober gazes on their faces, and I know that vigilance is a serious business.

"Watch and pray," Jesus told His followers, "so that you will not fall into temptation" (Mark 14:38). He wants me to stand guard over my own heart and remain alert for my soul's enemies, especially those areas where the enemy seems to ambush me again and again. Instead of racing frantically through each day, why not stop as these soldiers have done, and take a broader view of the weeks and months ahead and prayerfully prepare for whatever challenges might be coming down the road? As a confessed worrier, I know that always being on the lookout for danger can make me nervous and fearful. That's why I need to heed the advice "Devote yourselves to prayer, being watchful and thankful" (Colossians 4:2). Coupling watchfulness with thankfulness changes my perspective, taking the focus off of the threat and placing it on our living Saviour, who has kept watch over me in the past. As I observe the young soldiers at this modern watchtower, I also realize that my gaze has been turned inward for much too long. God wants us to watch out for one another, being vigilant in prayer, sounding a warning when we see someone in danger.

It's a watchman's duty and his responsibility to warn of approaching danger. In Old Testament times, most cities and towns had fortified walls and towers. The citizens posted watchmen on the walls, instructing them to remain alert day and night. The safety of the community was their responsibility. God appointed the prophet Ezekiel to be a watchman for his people, a task not to be taken lightly. He told him, "When I say to a wicked man, 'You will surely die,' and you do not warn him or speak out to dissuade him from his evil ways in order to save his life, that wicked man will die for his sin, and I will hold you accountable for his blood" (Ezekiel 3:18). In the same way, these young soldiers would be held accountable if they saw danger in the distance through their binoculars and shrugged it off.

It sounds harsh to punish the watchman, but this verse from Ezekiel shows us the heart of God. He doesn't want "anyone to perish, but everyone to come to repentance" (2 Peter 3:9). Do I understand the seriousness of my responsibility to warn others of the danger they are in, the deadly enemy stalking them? Do I feel the same sense of urgency and somber responsibility that Ezekiel and these soldiers demonstrate? If we're Christ's followers, we need to have the same heart that He does for the lost. We need to make use of the powerful equipment He has given us, the Holy Spirit, to find ways to warn people of the consequences of rejecting Him.

The apostle Paul told us to "Be on your guard; stand firm in the faith; be men of courage; be strong." Then he added, "Do everything in love" (1 Corinthians 16:13–14). And that's the most important part, I think. It's not enough for me to warn people of the dangers of a life of sin, but I must do it in a loving way. I want to be able to love sinners—I have to be able to love them—before I condemn their sin. Otherwise, why would they listen to me? Without genuine love I will be perceived as judgmental, a stereotypical, hypocritical Christian, pointing an accusing finger. And my warning will go unheeded.

Perhaps my first prayer should be for a deeper love and compassion for others, a heart like God's own that looks beyond the outward sin and sees individuals the way that He does. Before I start sounding a warning, I need to earn the right to be heard through acts of love and kindness.

I have some work to do when I get home. These soldiers at the watchtower have reminded me that God cares about people who are in danger with no one to warn them. Our job as the body of Christ is to keep watch, as if an unseen enemy is sneaking up on us. Because one is.

Joppa

We have come to the ancient Israeli seaport of Joppa on the Mediterranean Sea. Ships from all over the region once docked here, bringing exotic cargoes, their sailors babbling a multitude of languages. We have to wind through a maze of narrow streets to reach the waterfront, but suddenly the sea opens up in front of us, as blue and sparkling as a bowl of sapphires. Gentle waves curl against the shore as if beckoning shyly to us to set sail. I always feel hopeful when I'm near the sea, and also a little restless, longing to travel.

A whimsical statue of a whale reminds us of Joppa's claim to fame as the port from which the prophet Jonah sailed before being swallowed by a great fish. God called Jonah to preach to the Assyrians in Nineveh but he sailed in the opposite direction—and I don't blame him. The Assyrians were a brutal, violent people who enjoyed torturing their victims, prolonging death as long as possible. They were Israel's bitterest enemy, ruthlessly conquering the ten northern tribes and carrying them away into slavery. God wanted Jonah to preach to these vicious, godless pagans? Why not ask a Jew to go to Berlin at the height of Nazi power and preach to Adolf Hitler? Why not ask you and me to go to an Al Qaeda camp and preach the Gospel to Osama bin Laden's terrorists?

As soon as Jonah heard God's instructions, he headed here to Joppa to sail as far away from Nineveh as he possibly could. But it wasn't fear of the Assyrians that made him flee. After the storm nearly capsized Jonah's ship, after the sailors threw him overboard, and after he spent three days and nights in the belly of the great fish, Jonah confessed the true reason. "I knew you were merciful," he told God, "slow to anger and abounding in love" (see Jonah 4:2). Jonah's greatest fear was that God would forgive these enemies—and Jonah didn't want Him to.

God's command to preach to a Gentile nation shouldn't have come as a surprise to Jonah. Israel's calling as the Chosen People of God was to be a blessing to the non-Jewish world. The floor plan of God's Temple included a huge courtyard where Gentiles could come and worship. The Old Testament prophets and psalmists had promised that all nations would one day worship Israel's God. But Jonah wanted to be the one who decided which nations would be included in those promises and which ones wouldn't—and he definitely excluded the Assyrians! Joppa was the place where the prophet refused God's call.

The New Testament also mentions the port of Joppa. In Acts 10 we find the apostle Peter staying here with Simon the tanner, "whose house is by the sea" (v. 6). He probably enjoyed the same sunny view and gentle breezes that I'm enjoying. Peter had a powerful ministry here by the sea, teaching his fellow Jews about Jesus. He even raised a devout woman named Dorcas from the dead. But Peter, like Jonah, preached the Gospel only to Jews like himself. He was in a nice, comfortable, successful groove. Kind of like my own groove back home—or was it a rut?—before all the seismic changes began.

Peter's life got up-ended—like Jonah's and like mine did. In a vision, God told Peter to step out of his comfortable routine and kill and eat unclean animals. While Peter was still trying to comprehend the vision, messengers arrived from a Gentile centurion named Cornelius. The men begged Peter to come and preach the Gospel in the city of Caesarea—a Roman city with all of the cultural icons of Imperial Rome, such as an amphitheater, a hippodrome, and temples to pagan gods. Good Jewish men like Peter didn't visit Caesarea, and they certainly didn't eat non-kosher food in a Gentile home with uncircumcised centurions. But God's call had been very clear, the vision repeated three times in case Peter might be tempted to dismiss it as hunger pains: "Do not call anything impure that God has made clean" (Acts 10:15).

Cornelius was not only a Gentile but also a Roman. He was Peter's enemy, just as the Assyrians were Jonah's enemies. The Romans were ruthless pagans, too. I'm sure Peter hadn't forgotten how Roman soldiers had tortured and scourged and crucified Jesus while a Roman centurion stood by and watched. It's to Peter's credit that he didn't hop on the first freighter out of Joppa. But I don't think the irony of his situation would have been lost on him; God had called him to preach to his pagan enemies while visiting Joppa. I can almost see him smiling at God's timing. After all, Cornelius' messengers could have found Peter in one of the other towns he had visited. But no, they had come to him in Joppa. A further irony is that Peter's father was named Jonah. No one used last names, so Peter's official name was Peter the son of Jonah.

Peter obeyed God and went with these messengers to a Gentile household in a Roman city. As he preached, the pagans became believers. At last, God's Chosen People were fulfilling the promise made to Abraham that through them the whole world would be blessed.

Jesus had told the Jews who were seeking a miraculous sign that only "the sign of Jonah" would be given. "For as Jonah was three days and three nights in the belly of a huge fish, so the Son of Man will be three days and three nights in the heart of the earth" (Matthew 12:40). Jesus fulfilled this sign through His resurrection after three days in the tomb. But I think "the sign of Jonah" also might have been a reminder to the Jews—and to us—that God's mercy and loving-kindness at Calvary extend to all mankind, even our enemies.

Once Jonah returned to land and finally followed through on God's call, the Assyrians repented and came to faith, everyone from the king to the common man. The Jews of Jonah's day never would have believed it could happen. They didn't really want it to happen. Enemies belonged in the darkest corner of hell. And the Jews of Peter's day never would have believed that the enemy nation of Rome with its belief in a multitude of pagan gods would ever accept Christ and turn to the God of Israel. But they did. Peter eventually became the leader of the church in Rome. And Rome later became the headquarters of the Christian church.

Until my life began to change in unwanted ways, I was very comfortable living in my quiet, homogenous community in the peaceful Midwest. I liked my old, familiar ministries, writing Christian books, speaking at Christian churches and retreats and conferences. Like Jonah and Peter, I worked among people just like myself.

But two years ago, a huge mosque was built in my town, less than a mile from my house. I can see its golden dome from my bedroom window. With a local place to worship, Muslims are now moving here in large numbers. Muslim families purchased all three houses that recently sold on my street. They are now my neighbors. I haven't heard a direct call from God to minister to them other than the normal neighborliness—when the Muslim woman across the street couldn't get her car started last winter, my husband went over with jumper cables and helped her. But what if I did hear a more specific call? As I look out at the sea here in Joppa, I wonder how I would respond. Would I go immediately like Peter did, or sail the other way like Jonah? Would I remember that it wasn't Jonah's and Peter's preaching skills that brought repentance and faith to unbelievers, but the work of the Holy Spirit?

I take a photograph of the Mediterranean Sea to hang over my desk back home, reminding me that Joppa is a place of decision, a place where God demonstrates His great love for all mankind. I shouldn't be surprised if I find myself there. Nor should I be surprised if He asks me to put aside my fear and prejudice and look at people—even those I might consider enemies—and see them the way He does.

I smile at God's sense of humor—and my own naiveté for believing that I really have a choice. Jonah's escape was temporary. God has very creative ways of steering us back to His planned destination and purpose. Hopefully it won't take three nights in a whale's belly to convince me that I'm headed in the wrong direction. I may be uncomfortable with one-on-one evangelism or a change in my usual routine, but I'm also a very poor swimmer. I prefer to do my whale watching from a distance.

The Aqueduct at Caesarea

We have traveled some thirty miles up the coast from Joppa to a beautiful stretch of beach on the Mediterranean Sea. The water beneath cloudless skies is a deep indigo blue, the waves tipped with silver. I have shucked my shoes and peeled off my socks to walk in the warm sand. But the beach isn't the main attraction here. Between me and the gently lapping surf are the remains of a two-thousand-year-old Roman aqueduct. The trestle marches along the shore in a long, precise line like a regiment of Roman soldiers. The sandy stones from which it is built are the same color as the beach—as if something this monumental could be camouflaged. We pose for pictures beneath one of the sturdy arches that support the water channel high above our heads. Two young people ignore the warning signs and scale the two-story structure to stand on top, waving.

Like the tourists all around me, I "ooh" and "ahh" over the aqueduct, snapping multiple photographs. It's so old! So graceful! A marvel of engineering! I'm not surprised to learn that the man who constructed it is none other than King Herod. He needed this aqueduct to bring fresh drinking water from a spring on top of Mount Carmel to his port city of Caesarea—a distance of twelve miles. The aqueduct is no longer completely intact, but the remaining structure impresses all of us.

When we finish admiring this wonder, we clean the sand off our feet and climb back into the bus for the short ride to Caesarea, where we quickly discover that the aqueduct is just one of many engineering feats. King Herod wanted a thoroughly Roman city on Israel's coast, a world-class administrative center to serve as his capital with all of the comforts of Rome. He wanted easy access to the Mediterranean for shipping and travel, but his chosen site not only lacked adequate drinking water, it lacked a natural port. Neither obstacle stopped him. Along with the twelve-mile-long aqueduct, he also built a harbor. His engineers constructed huge underwater supports for a breakwater using hydraulic concrete, and then adorned the entrance to the man-made port with enormous statues. Remnants of the breakwater are still visible in the clear water offshore, shimmering beneath the surface like a mirage. Herod's arrogance reminds me of the men of ancient Babel who said, "Let us build ourselves a city, with a tower that reaches to the heavens, so that we may make a name for ourselves" (Genesis 11:4).

Aqueduct

I could spend hours walking through the ruins of Caesarea, which was once the second-greatest city in the nation after Jerusalem. This thoroughly Roman showplace includes a 20,000-seat hippodrome for race fans, temples to everyone's favorite Roman gods, opulent bathhouses for relaxation, and a 4,000-seat amphitheater overlooking the Mediterranean Sea. I explore Herod's royal palace, perched near the shore, and dip my fingers in the remnants of his swimming pool, an authentic "infinity pool" that allowed swimmers to enjoy the view of the sea and the harbor. Chunks of white marble litter the ground where I walk, Carrera marble imported from Italy to adorn the buildings. And when I stand on the remains of the military garrison where the apostle Paul was likely imprisoned, I can't help wondering if he heard the sigh of the waves and the cries of sea birds from his cell or maybe the roar of the crowd from the hippodrome, the pounding of horses and chariot wheels.

But Herod's once-prosperous city disappeared from history, lying buried and forgotten beneath the Mediterranean sand for centuries before being excavated in modern times. When archaeologists analyzed the destruction patterns, they discovered that Caesarea was destroyed by an earthquake and the enormous tsunami that followed. I think of the Scripture verse, "Unless the Lord builds the house, its builders labor in vain. Unless the Lord watches over the city, the watchmen stand guard in vain" (Psalm 127:1).

King Herod's mind-set was a lot like our modern American one: If you can dream it, you can build it. Need a port in the middle of a barren coastline? No problem—just create one. Need a water supply for your new city? Simply build an aqueduct. Our Jewish guide tells us that his ancestors didn't need aqueducts because they were wise enough to build their cities near a water source. In the same way, he says, we need to build our lives around God's Word, staying close to it, safeguarding it, remembering that the true Source of life is God. The one who delights in God's Word will be "like a tree planted by streams of water. . . . Whatever he does prospers" (Psalm 1:3).

There is nothing wrong with dreaming big dreams or working hard to fulfill them as long as they are God's dreams for me and not creations of my selfish imagination. I have a habit of rushing ahead and making plans, then asking God to bless them—much like choosing a building site for a city only to discover that there is no water supply. This past year, I've grumbled at some of the hard places where God has put me—places that made me feel banished to a rocky outcropping on Mount Carmel, far from the pleasant shoreline and glittery city. I've tried to escape from such hard situations and searched for an easier, less painful place to settle—only to find myself dry and thirsty. But perhaps God, in His mercy and love, has put me in this barren place for reasons that only He can see. I may prefer a sandy beach or the excitement of Caesarea, but Mount Carmel has springs of fresh water—and it remained safe from the tidal wave that destroyed the city.

I think of Jesus' parable of the house on the rock, so familiar to us that we sometimes gloss over it, reducing it to a children's story, a Sunday school ditty. But I see how profound Christ's words are as I gaze around at the ruins of Caesarea. "Everyone who hears these words of mine and puts them into practice," Jesus said, "is like a wise man who built his house on the rock" (Matthew 7:24). If I'm living in obedience to the Word of God, then all of the floods and storms of life, like the ones I've been experiencing lately, will be unable to shake me. But if I've based my plans on something other than God's Word then I'm no better than King Herod or the foolish man who built his house on sand: "The rain came down, the streams rose, and the winds blew and beat against that house, and it fell with a great crash" (Matthew 7:27). When the storms blow and my own plans fall into ruins, I can look at the crumbling aqueduct, the remains of Caesarea, and understand why.

Mount Carmel, with its freshwater springs, is the place where Elijah confronted the false gods that the people of Israel were worshiping. "How long will you waver between two opinions?" Elijah asked them. "If the Lord is God, follow him; but if Baal is God, follow him" (1 Kings 18:21). So where do I want to live? In a place of pleasure and ease, serving the gods of our culture in order to avoid suffering? Or am I willing to live in a seemingly barren place as long as it's close to the Source of life?

The City of Shechem

Traveling north toward Galilee, we skirt the long ridge of mountains that run like a spine down the center of Israel.

These aren't imposing peaks like the Rockies or Alps, but a rumpled green carpet of hills, scrunched and scuffed and strewn with rocks. At night, we can spot the towns and villages by the chartreuse lights that shine from the tops of Muslim minarets.

Halfway between Jerusalem and Galilee, we come to the biblical city of Shechem nestled between two guardian peaks, Mount Ebal and Mount Gerizim. The city has been renamed *Nablus*, and it's in the heart of the occupied territories known as the West Bank. My palms start to sweat whenever we travel through non-Israeli towns, because no one can be certain if a busload of American tourists will be greeted by souvenir sellers or slingstones. In Jesus' day, the "greetings" in this territory were decidedly hostile. Shechem was in the heart of Samaritan territory, and a Samaritan temple once stood atop Mount Gerizim. Jews were as unwelcome back then as they are now. Yet Scripture says that Jesus visited Jacob's well near Shechem and had an extended conversation with a Samaritan woman.

In spite of my uneasiness at entering Palestinian territory, I'm eager to glimpse this site. It's little more than a dusty Middle Eastern town with a few archaeological ruins, but to me, it's a landmark place, the site of kept promises. In the book of Genesis, young Joseph set off in his multicolored coat on an errand for his father, searching for his brothers who were tending their flocks near Shechem. Joseph's hike was a long one—a distance of more than 44 miles from Bethlehem. And did I mention that this territory is mountainous? The transmission on our tour bus chugs and huffs like the Big Bad Wolf as it negotiates the hills and mountain passes, and I would growl, too, if I had to hike this route on foot. Joseph might have been relieved to finally see his brothers and their flocks in the distance, but his relief was short-lived. Burning with jealousy, his brothers attacked him and sold him into slavery in Egypt.

When my Jewish friends retell this story, they don't glamorize Joseph the way we do, seeing him as a victim of malicious older brothers. They see him as a selfish, spoiled brat who had a God-given dream that his brothers would one day bow down to him, and who then acted to bring it about himself, becoming a snitch, a tattletale. Before God could fulfill His promise and raise Joseph up, Joseph would first have to go down into slavery and exile and suffering.

At times Joseph must have believed he would die, first in the pit where his brothers threw him, and later in prison in Egypt. How could God's purpose for his life ever be fulfilled under these circumstances? But while Joseph may have doubted his future, he didn't give up on God. Perhaps as he lay in prison replaying his ill-fated journey to Shechem, he recalled the promise that God had made to his ancestor Abraham in that very city. Shechem was the first place Abraham stopped in the Promised Land and built an altar to God. And it's where God made the promise, "To your offspring I will give this land" (Genesis 12:7). At the time, Abraham had a barren wife, no offspring, and didn't own any real estate in this land, which already happened to be inhabited. Later Joseph's father, Jacob, also built an altar in Shechem. He had sojourned in exile for a long time, trying to grab God's promises through his own ingenuity until Jacob finally bowed to the God of his ancestors, vowing to serve Him (Genesis 33:20).

Joseph must have kept these stories in mind, because after everything he endured, after finally accomplishing God's plan for his life, he asked his descendants to carry his bones back from Egypt to the Promised Land and bury them in Shechem—the place where his long, dark journey into slavery began. Maybe this was Joseph's way of saying, "My enemies thought they'd defeated me here, that God's purpose for my life was derailed, but God always keeps His promises."

Four hundred years after Joseph was carried off to Egypt, God delivered the entire nation from slavery and they brought Joseph's bones home during the exodus (Exodus 13:19). Moses' successor, Joshua, buried those bones at Shechem (Joshua 24:32). The Promised Land had been conquered by Israel, the people settled in the land. God's promise to Abraham had come true—the land was theirs—and so Joshua assembled the nation here at Shechem. With half of the people standing on the slopes of Mount Gerizim, the other half on Mount Ebal, he recounted the miracles that God had performed for them, how He'd led them and guided them. Joshua told the people, "You know with all your heart and soul that not one of all the good promises the Lord your God gave you has failed. Every promise has been fulfilled; not one has failed" (Joshua 23:14). Joshua ended his speech with the stirring words, "Choose for yourselves this day whom you will serve . . . But as for me and my household, we will serve the Lord" (Joshua 24:15).

And that's the choice we must make each day, especially when, like Joseph, we find ourselves forced to go in a direction other than the one we have chosen, walking a path of suffering. Will I continue to trust that God's plan for me will be fulfilled even though I have to wait for it like Abraham did, like Joseph did—and then wait some more? Will I choose to believe that God has a purpose for all the detours in my life?

We can pick any one of the hundreds of promises that we have in Christ and claim it as our own, knowing that God always keeps His promises. Always. Not one has failed. The fact that I'm standing here in Shechem, a forgiven, beloved child of God, is the fulfillment of another promise that God gave to Abraham, saying that through him, all the people on earth would be blessed (Genesis 12:3). Not only the Jews but also the Gentiles could become His children—a prophecy that was fulfilled through Christ. After Jesus had His conversation here with the woman at the well, "Many of the Samaritans from that town believed in him" (John 4:39). They were Gentiles—and God's promise of worldwide blessing began to be fulfilled.

God's Word is as firm and sure as these two mountains that stand guard above this place. I can choose to believe—and trust and wait, knowing that God always keeps His promises. Or I can take matters into my own hands and try to fulfill them on my own, like Joseph initially did. Today, I choose once again to trust Him, in spite of all the unsettling changes back home, in spite of the dryness I've felt in my soul. My calling hasn't changed and neither has God. I am called to be His workmanship—His one-of-a-kind masterpiece—"created in Christ Jesus to do good works, which God prepared in advance for us to do" (Ephesians 2:10). He is not only interested in what I do for Him, but also in the person I am becoming in the process. The God who changed childless Abraham into the father of many nations, who changed Joseph from a spoiled brat into a world leader, and who transformed the unhappy woman at the well into His daughter, wants to transform me, too.

The lesson of Shechem is that God is faithful. The question we all face when we stand here—like Abraham once did—is will I choose to believe His promises?

For as high as the heavens are above the earth, so great is his love for those who fear him; as far as the east is from the west, so far has he removed our transgressions from us.

Psalm 103:11–12

A NEW PRAYER FOR THE JOURNEY

Our faithful, promise-keeping Father,

I praise You for Your unfailing love and mercy for all mankind, a love that we cannot imagine and don't deserve. Not one of Your good promises to us have failed, nor will they ever fail. Forgive me for stubbornly running from Your call, like Jonah, when asked to share Your love with others. You have taken me to hard, dry places in order to break my sinful habits and reveal my need to change, yet I have resisted. Thank You, Lord, for this dry season and for all You are teaching me through it. Keep me watchful against unseen enemies, against compromise, and may I be faithful to sound the warning and to fight Your battles with courage. Help me to hear Your call and, like Peter, to walk unafraid into the work You have chosen for me to do.

Amen

9

GALILEE

Jesus returned to Galilee in the power of the Spirit, and news
about him spread through the whole countryside. He taught
in their synagogues, and everyone praised him.

Luke 4:14–15

We have reached the region of Galilee and the shimmering, harp-shaped lake that's known as the Sea of Galilee. Jesus and His disciples had to be rugged indeed to walk all the way here from Jerusalem. I'm tired after the long bus ride! The lake is smaller than most people imagine; you can see the opposite shore no matter which side you stand on. But I love that the Galilee region is green even though the calendar says it's winter. It feels like paradise after the brutal wilderness in the south. This is an area of orchards and vineyards, banana groves, citrus trees, and avocado farms. Our bus drives past a lemon grove and the bright yellow fruit seems to glow against the dark green leaves.

We finally climb off the bus, and I am awestruck to find myself standing in the biblical village of Capernaum. It's one of those places I've heard about in Sunday school lessons and in sermons all of my life but never imagined I would visit. The name, so mispronounced in Christian circles, was originally "K'far Nahum" meaning "Village of Nahum"—possibly the prophet's birthplace. The town rests on the shore of the Sea of Galilee, and the sun seems brighter here as it reflects off the water. It's a beautiful lake, the same one that Jesus saw.

Jesus used Capernaum as the headquarters for His ministry. "Leaving Nazareth, [Jesus] went and lived in Capernaum, which was by the lake in the area of Zebulun and Naphtali" (Matthew 4:13). It was also the hometown of His disciples Peter and Andrew, and their fishing partners James and John. There is no longer a village of any kind here, only Israel's typical tourist combination of archaeological ruins and a Christian church commemorating the site.

The most impressive set of ruins are those of a spacious synagogue dating from the fourth or fifth century AD. This building wasn't here in Jesus' day, but it stands on the foundation of the one that was. The synagogue where Jesus taught would have looked much like this one, with the same features common to all synagogues in Galilee. Tall stone pillars held up the roof of the sanctuary, and steplike seats lined three of its walls like bleachers, facing the flat area in the middle. A special niche contained the sacred scrolls of the Law and the Prophets. Outside, a *mikveh*, or ritual bath, would have been used for purification.

Jesus preached here, on this very spot: "They went to Capernaum, and when the Sabbath came, Jesus went into the synagogue and began to teach. The people were amazed

Jerusalem Church

at his teaching, because he taught them as one who had authority, not as the teachers of the law" (Mark 1:21–22). It's easy to picture Him standing in the center of the synagogue floor, reading from the Torah, explaining God's Word to the people as they sat in rapt attention. The gospel of John records one of Jesus' more controversial sermons, which included the startling words: "Whoever eats my flesh and drinks my blood has eternal life . . ." (6:54). John concludes by noting, "He said this while teaching in the synagogue in Capernaum" (John 6:59). Yes, this site has authenticity, a sense that Jesus was here, and that lives were forever changed in this place.

"As soon as they left the synagogue, they went with James and John to the home of Simon and Andrew" (Mark 1:29). Capernaum was a very small village and it's a short walk from the synagogue to the remains of Peter's home. After Jesus arrived, He cured Simon Peter's mother-in-law of a fever, and she got out of bed to wait on Him. Later that same evening when the Sabbath ended, "The whole town gathered

at the door, and Jesus healed many who had various diseases"
(vv. 33–34).

Peter was a fisherman, and his home was a humble stone
dwelling where several generations probably lived under one
roof. In this temperate Mediterranean climate, much of the
cooking and other daily living would have taken place in the
outdoor courtyard. Archaeologists identified these ruins as
Peter's house because of a very early Christian church that had
been built over the remains of a first-century home. Another
church from the fifth century was built on top of that one.
Both churches are gone. Today, Peter's house is barely visible
beneath a modern church that looks as though a spaceship
has landed on Peter's roof.

What strikes me about Capernaum is that it is nothing
more than a tourist site. The small, present-day churches that
mark the site appear to be tourist destinations, not thriving
congregations. The once-bustling fishing village—the home
base of the Son of God and His ministry—is gone. Just as
Jesus warned it would be. "Woe to you, Korazin! Woe to
you, Bethsaida! For if the miracles that were performed in
you had been performed in Tyre and Sidon, they would have
repented . . . And you, Capernaum, will you be lifted up to the
skies? No, you will go down to the depths" (Luke 10:13, 15).
If it weren't for the ruins, you wouldn't know that the town
had existed. The village from Jesus' day, like so many other
sites in Israel, was destroyed during the Roman invasion in
AD 70 that also demolished the Temple and Jerusalem. An
earthquake or one of many foreign invaders over the past two
thousand years probably razed the fifth-century synagogue
that was rebuilt over the original one. Israel has seen much
destruction and warfare since Jesus' day, including six wars

since the founding of the modern nation in 1948. I'm not surprised that nothing much is left.

I wonder, as I walk through the remains of Capernaum, if God allowed the turmoil and upheaval for a reason. The early Christians might have been tempted to build a huge institution on this site. This was Jesus' headquarters, after all. Why not make it the Christian church's headquarters, too? Why not build a sprawling religious campus with a 4,000-seat auditorium and a ministry center and a healing hospital and a discipleship training school? The apostles could have sat back and waited for the world to flock here to learn from them. Why not use Capernaum to launch all of the programs and ministries that the church has founded in His name over the centuries?

The early Christians might have done exactly that if they had been given the choice. Instead, God allowed chaos and destruction, persecution and scattering. It began, we're told in Acts 11, after Stephen was stoned to death. But instead of destroying the young Christian church, the chaos and desolation at the end of the first century strengthened it. Scattered against their will, the early Christians brought the teachings of Jesus to the entire world. They became salt, scattered freely, and light, shining abundantly, everywhere they went.

It might be our natural tendency to build impressive monuments for Christian ministry, but it isn't God's way. We are supposed to go out into the world, not wait for the world to come to us, even if God has to turn our comfortable lives upside down to get us to do it. I'm told that in the original Greek language, the wording of Jesus' Great Commission reads: "*As you are going* into the world . . . make disciples." Jesus assumes that we will be going; His orders are to make disciples along the way. When He sent His disciples out two by two to teach in all of the villages, He didn't tell them to buy a chunk of land and build an impressive building. He said, "Take nothing for the journey except a staff—no bread, no bag, no money in your belts" (Mark 6:8). I call that traveling light. Jesus wanted them to trust God and the Holy Spirit's leading, not build elaborate projects and programs and ministries.

I've learned, here in Capernaum, not to get too comfortable. When my world is shaken and my ministry seems to change and I'm forced to move on, it doesn't mean that something is wrong in my life. This is God's usual way of doing things. His template is change, not settling down. It's a relief to know that the upheaval I've been experiencing is normal. I can trust Him. In the long run, His building plans always turn out so much better than mine.

The Decapolis

Now, this is a city! I have come to the ruins of Scythopolis, one of the ten settlements known in Scripture as the Decapolis. These free Roman cities were located within the borders of Israel but were inhabited by Gentiles, not Jews. Roman culture and customs flourished here. In Jesus' day, Scythopolis was located at the crossroads of two main travel routes, one going through the Jezreel Valley to the Mediterranean coast, the other following the Jordan Valley north to Galilee or south to Jerusalem.

Today Scythopolis is a ghost town, the casualty of an earthquake. But the excavations and reconstructions are so widespread, so nearly complete, it's easy to see I'm walking through a once-bustling city. I stroll down colonnaded streets adorned with monumental pillars. I enter a row of boutique-sized shops paved with intricate mosaic floors. I peek into a pagan temple and then a Roman-style bathhouse rivaling any modern spa. Near the amphitheater, there is even a public bathroom with indoor toilets, the space large enough to serve as a modern rest stop along a major highway. I walk through the arched entrance to the theater and climb the stone bleachers to the "nosebleed" section. The acoustics are so perfect that when four students from our group stand on the stage and sing, their voices carry all the way up to where I'm sitting, as clearly as if they used microphones. Tourists in the gift shop on the hill behind the amphitheater come out to listen.

As a practicing Jew, Jesus probably never spent much time here in Scythopolis, if He visited at all. Devout Jews who followed the teachings of the Torah avoided places like this, with its Roman decadence and idolatry. The cities of the Decapolis were pockets of foreign, pagan culture invading the Jews' ancestral land; Gentiles built their own cities and Jews built theirs. You don't find synagogues or ritual baths in the Decapolis, nor do you find pagan temples and Roman baths in small Jewish towns. Jesus and His disciples would have looked very conspicuous here among the toga-draped Romans, easily identifiable as religious Jews with their beards and head coverings and ritual tassels dangling from their garments.

Although Jesus may have stayed away from Scythopolis, Scripture says that large crowds from the Decapolis followed Him (Matthew 4:25). What drew them? Was He a curiosity, the latest celebrity to chase for their own amusement? As word of His healing miracles spread, some people probably followed

Him in search of a cure. But how many of Scythopolis' citizens gave up their Roman gods and bathhouses and other amusements to become Christians? The Bible doesn't say.

As I tour modern Israel, it's still pretty easy to tell which Jews are Orthodox and which are not. Religious men still wear beards and head coverings and tassels on the corners of their garments. Religious women dress conservatively with long sleeves, long hemlines, and high necklines. I can't help wondering what our tour group looks like to them. Can they tell by looking at us that we're Christians? I have seen Orthodox men avert their gaze as the young women in our group parade by in tank tops and plunging necklines, and I shudder at the message we're sending.

Christians are difficult to spot in our culture, blending in so well that we're indistinguishable from typical Americans. A cross dangling from a necklace has become such a common decoration that it's no longer an indicator of the wearer's faith. Jesus said that His followers "are not of the world any more than I am of the world" (John 17:14), but how do we draw that line, separating ourselves from the popular culture without becoming bogged down in legalism? Should we stand out in a crowd or shouldn't we?

The Old Testament gave Jews very specific guidelines on how to dress, including the way men should cut their beards. Likewise, the New Testament gives guidelines to Christians, advising among other things for "women to dress modestly, with decency and propriety" (1 Timothy 2:9). But even more emphasis is given in Scripture to our character and to our actions. We shouldn't fit comfortably in a godless culture any more than Jesus could fit comfortably in Scythopolis. I should feel uneasy in an environment that flouts God's moral principles and takes His name in vain. I shouldn't be desensitized to movies and TV shows that are violent and sacrilegious and profane. They should shock me. We're told to focus our minds on things that are true and noble and pure and admirable (Philippians 4:8). I can't avoid being surrounded by our popular culture, but I can be careful not to adopt its habits and world view. We're told to be in this world but not of it.

Jesus traveled through the region where I'm now sitting, not to absorb their habits and culture or even to condemn them, but to minister God's love and grace. People were important to Him, so important that He would stop His travel plans to speak with them and heal them. So maybe I should ask myself this question: Is the love of Christ evident in my life, or am I indistinguishable from the rest of the crowd? I hardly think it would matter if I dressed like an Amish woman and cloistered myself from the "bad" stuff in our culture if my actions and words were just like everyone else's. "The kingdom of God is within you," Jesus said (Luke 17:21). I take Christ's forgiveness and grace wherever I go. In my day-to-day life, the way I treat the bank teller and the grocery clerk and the mail carrier all matter. My reaction to the guy who cuts me off in traffic or steals my parking spot matters. So does the way I treat members of my extended family who don't know Christ. In the words of the old gospel song, "They will know we are Christians by our love."

Two thousand years ago, some of the people from Scythopolis who sat where I'm now sitting laced on their sandals and went looking for Jesus. For many, it must have been like following the latest celebrity to see what the fuss was all about. But there might have been one or two people who were tired of their vain, empty lives and longed for words of life and healing for their souls. Maybe one of the people I encounter every day longs for the same thing. In our culture of busyness, people are often secondary to results and things. Why not go countercultural, laying aside my busy agenda and to-do lists to put people first? And while I'm rubbing shoulders with the world, I can show them the love of Christ.

God has placed us at the busy crossroads of our culture for a reason. He wants all of our actions and attitudes in all of our petty, everyday affairs to be so different, so transformed by His grace, that we stand out from the crowd—as conspicuous as a religious Jew in ancient Scythopolis. He wants you and me to "let your light shine before men, that they may see your good deeds and praise your Father in heaven" (Matthew 5:16).

City on a Hill

I'm relaxing on the balcony of my hotel room on a balmy evening, gazing at a stunning view of the Sea of Galilee. The night sky is pricked by millions of stars, the air scented with tropical foliage that rustles gently in the breeze. From my vantage point, the sea looks like a bowl of molten silver surrounded by hills of rumpled green velvet. On one of the hills across the lake from me, the city of Tiberias twinkles and shines, its lights reflected and multiplied on the still water.

I love Galilee. Jesus spent so much time preaching here, visiting towns and villages all over this area, that it feels like I'm walking in His footsteps and hearing echoes of His voice everywhere I go. And the firefly lights of Tiberias remind me of His words, "A city on a hill cannot be hidden." I pull out my Bible and find the verse. It's part of His Sermon on the Mount and was probably delivered on the slope of a hill not far from Tiberias. But as I read, I'm surprised to discover what the complete verse says: "You are the light of the world. A city on a hill cannot be hidden" (Matthew 5:14). He's talking to us.

I remembered Jesus saying that *He* was the light of the world, but I had forgotten that He said *we* were the light of the world, too. He didn't say "You *will* be" or "You *should* be," He said that we *are*. He isn't shaking His finger at us or encouraging us to decide, like the children's song to "Hide it under a bushel? No! I'm gonna let it shine." He's telling us the way it is, and these are the facts: If I'm His disciple, then I am the light of the world. And as clearly as I can see Tiberias glowing in the dark ten miles away, my light cannot be hidden. Furthermore, Jesus says that since I'm already shining out there in plain sight, I should let my light shine before men in a way that brings glory to God (v. 16).

When Christ walked these hills by the Sea of Galilee, He shone God's light into all of the dark places. The author of Matthew's gospel realized that Jesus was fulfilling Isaiah's prophecy: "In the past [God] humbled the land of Zebulun and the land of Naphtali, but in the future he will honor Galilee of the Gentiles, by the way of the sea, along the Jordan— The people walking in darkness have seen a great light; on those living in the land of the shadow of death a light has dawned" (Isaiah 9:1–2; see Matthew 4:13–16). In Isaiah's lifetime the brutal Assyrian army invaded this region, and the inhabitants of Galilee were the first in Israel to be slaughtered or carried off as slaves into exile. Darkness and the shadow of death surely covered this place. But Isaiah foresaw a time when a great light would dawn: "For to us a child is born, to us a son is given . . . And he will be called Wonderful Counselor,

Mighty God, Everlasting Father, Prince of Peace" (9:6). The first place that had suffered captivity was now being set free through Christ's ministry.

It's inspiring to read those Scriptures and see God at work, faithfully fulfilling His Word. But I'm part of that prophetic picture, as well. God's light dawned with Christ and now shines in me and through me. I'm supposed to light up a world that is lost, shining like a city on a hill. Men and women whom God loves are groping in darkness, searching for the way. I know a few of them! God placed the light of Christ within us because He wants us to illuminate the path for those who are lost.

The only thing worse than being lost and unable to find your way is being lost in the dark. Once, on a family camping trip in Canada, Ken and I and our children foolishly set off for a hike in the woods after supper—without flashlights—thinking we could return to our campsite before dark. But we misjudged the length and difficulty of the trail, and we were still deep in the woods when night fell. The path became increasingly harder to follow in the dark, our progress slower. The kids began to panic, imagining bears and wildcats and being lost in the vast Canadian wilderness forever. Okay, I confess—I was spooked, too. Just as the kids' fears were turning into tears, we spotted a faint light winking among the trees. We hurried toward it—after convincing our daughter that bears didn't carry flashlights—and we soon saw more lights, flickering inside tents and glowing in campfires. Praise God, we had found the campground! We weren't going to die after all!

That's the visual picture Scripture is drawing for us. Jesus said that you and I are those lights shining in the darkness, giving hope to people who are lost and fearful, lighting their way home to Christ. Whoever follows Him "will never walk in darkness, but will have the light of life" (John 8:12). True, we might have to walk through fearful places. And we may make some unwise choices on our journey or fail to pay attention to the dimming light. But with Christ as our guide, at least we will see where we're going instead of wandering around lost. We may even spot another city on a hill to help guide our steps.

Before I leave this balcony and go to bed for the night, I take one last lingering look at the lights on the hill across from me. I am that city! I need to crawl out of the rut I've been digging back home and look for a hill to climb so I can shine. Hide my light under a bushel? No. Not when there are so many dark places in this world that need God's light.

The Mount of the Beatitudes

The Church of the Beatitudes perches like a queen on top of a hill overlooking the Sea of Galilee. Far below us, the lake looks serene, dotted with a half dozen boats. According to tradition, this is the mountainside where Jesus taught the lessons we call the Sermon on the Mount, including the Beatitudes. It's easy to visualize Jesus seated here beneath an azure sky, His followers spread out on the slope, which acted as a natural amphitheater to amplify His voice. It's quiet here, miles from the nearest city, and the church's beautifully landscaped grounds seem to invite prayer and meditation. Our guide reads portions of the sermon to us, then invites us to find a spot to sit alone for a while and contemplate Jesus' words.

I choose a low stone wall beneath a tree and sit facing the Sea of Galilee, the sun warming my face. I try to hear Jesus' words the way His original audience did, as if for the first time. I'm especially struck by the portion of the sermon where Jesus gives the Old Testament Law a new spin: You have heard it said do not murder, but I say don't even harbor anger in your heart. You have heard it said do not commit adultery, but I say don't even let your heart long for someone who isn't your spouse. You have heard it said love your neighbor, but I say love your enemies and pray for them (see Matthew 5). Jesus raised the bar even higher for us, saying that outward conformity to the Law isn't enough: "For I tell you that unless your righteousness surpasses that of the Pharisees and the teachers of the law, you will certainly not enter the kingdom of heaven" (Matthew 5:20). It's what's inside our heart that counts.

This new, harder standard is part of the new covenant that God made with us through Christ: "I will put my law in their minds and write it on their hearts. I will be their God, and they will be my people. . . . They will all know me, from the least of them to the greatest" (Jeremiah 31:33–34). The Pharisees counted 613 Old Testament laws that Jews had to keep in order to be considered righteous. As impossible as this seemed, at least they could compare their behavior to a standard and see whether or not they measured up. The rich young ruler could sincerely assure Jesus that he had faithfully kept all of the laws since his youth. But Jesus is saying that keeping the letter of the Law isn't enough. The outward conformity that the Pharisees demanded isn't enough. It's what's in your heart that matters. The rich young ruler was outwardly obedient, but in his heart he clung to his wealth. Jesus' words undoubtedly shook up a lot of people.

I can look at the Ten Commandments and say that "technically" I haven't broken any of them. But using the standard that Jesus gives, I have probably broken all ten of them! I've been explosively angry with people at times, assaulting them with vicious, killing words. And what about the command not to covet? I would have to stop watching TV ads and reading magazines and window-shopping at the mall in order to stop coveting. I would have to stop jealously comparing my friends' lives and ministries with my own. How can I ever measure up to Christ's standards of purity of heart?

God wants me to follow His rules out of a deep, heartfelt love for Him, out of gratitude for His grace, out of a desire to please Him more than myself. God wants a relationship with me, not rule-keeping. He sent His Holy Spirit into my life to show me what's in my heart and to convict me—if I really want to hear it, if I'm willing to let Him peer inside all the hidden places. Do I really want to be changed from the inside out, or do I consider myself already good enough?

I grow uncomfortable as I ponder these unsettling thoughts—and it's not from the rocky perch I'm sitting on. It occurs to me that King David, who broke at least two of the Ten Commandments when he committed adultery with Bathsheba and then conspired to kill her husband, was called "a man after God's own heart." Maybe it's because David turned to God for mercy and was willing to pray, "Search me, O God, and know my heart . . . See if there is any offensive way in me" (Psalm 139:23–24). David is commended throughout Scripture as a man of God, yet Jesus condemned the "holy men" of His age, the Pharisees and teachers of the Law, saying, "You clean the outside of the cup and dish, but inside they are full of greed and self-indulgence" (Matthew

23:25). He desires that His laws be written on our hearts, not tallied up in rule books and ledgers.

At last, our guide calls for our group to regather. The sun feels even warmer now as he leads us on a hike down the sloping hillside toward the Sea of Galilee. I continue to pray and search my heart as I go. The path winds through a leafy banana grove, and we see bunches of ripening bananas, still attached to the tree, that have been sealed in plastic bags to protect them. If only our hearts could be sealed that way against sin. I begin to hum an old hymn as I walk, singing the words in my mind:

> Prone to wander, Lord, I feel it,
> Prone to leave the God I love;
> Here's my heart, O take and seal it;
> Seal it for Thy courts above.

My knees feel wobbly from descending the steep slope when we finally reach the lakeshore, some forty minutes later. We've come to a narrow, rock-strewn beach, the traditional place where Christ appeared to His disciples after His resurrection and cooked a breakfast of fish. Peter and the others had returned to their old profession of fishing. What else could Peter do? He had denied that he even knew Jesus and must have thought he no longer deserved to be His disciple. Peter had been disappointed in the way things had turned out, thinking he had signed up for a rebellion against Rome, that the Messiah would rule over a physical kingdom, and that he would hold a position of honor. Yet as Peter and Jesus ate breakfast on the beach that morning, two things happened between them: Peter repented and accepted Jesus' forgiveness for his failures and denials, and then he accepted Jesus' commission to be His disciple again. This time he would follow God's plans for the kingdom, not his own.

I sink down on the sand to pray. I'm as guilty as Peter was of following my own plans, not God's. I had decided what my life as a disciple should look like, what my role in the kingdom should be, and then I became angry and depressed when things didn't turn out the way I thought they should. I've been careful to be a good little Christian on the outside while sometimes allowing sin to fester in my heart.

I ask God to forgive me for coveting, for jealously looking at my friends who have their children and grandchildren living nearby and wanting what they have instead of what I have been given. I ask God to forgive me for not trusting Him, not embracing change. My greatest sin has been unbelief, doubting the goodness of God, doubting that the changes He brought into my life will be for my good, and not for harm.

I confess my sin to Him. I accept His forgiveness. Then I accept the role of His disciple once again, no matter where it may take me in the future. I embrace the changes that God has brought into my life. Then, like Peter, I stand up and brush the sand off my clothes. I walk away from the beach, forgiven. And I begin again.

Walking on Water

From the safety of our vehicle parked on a mountaintop, we watch as a sudden thunderstorm rumbles toward the Sea of Galilee. Lightning flashes, black clouds tumble and roll, thunder booms. Within minutes, icy sheets of rain are lashing our windows as the wind rocks the vehicle. A group of hikers, fleeing to their car, have difficulty standing upright. The gale snatches a woman's umbrella, sucking it inside out, reducing it to a worthless tangle of metal and cloth. The storm has descended so quickly that one minute we were looking down at the tranquil sea, admiring the view, and the next minute we were running for cover. I've read in Scripture about sudden storms on the Sea of Galilee, storms that Jesus miraculously calmed, but now I understand how seasoned fishermen like Peter, James, and John could have been caught by surprise out on the open water.

In a storm like this one, Peter walked on water. It was also in the dark of night. Why not give water-walking lessons on a sunny day with calm seas? All of the disciples could have joined in the fun. Crowds of sightseers could have watched from shore, marveling at the miracle. Peter's non-believing friends and relatives finally would have understood why he'd chosen to abandon the family fishing business to follow a wandering, homeless rabbi. Instead, darkness obscured the disciples' vision, fear filled their hearts. They'd been rowing all night, expending great effort, and still were far from shore. Waves threatened to swamp the boat, drowning all of them.

Then, out of the wind and darkness, Jesus appeared, striding calmly across the surface of the lake. At first the disciples were terrified, but Jesus assured them, "It is I. Don't be afraid." I'm not sure what came over Peter at that moment, but he boldly replied, "Lord, if it's you . . . tell me to come to you on the water."

Jesus said, "Come" (see Matthew 14:22–32).

Ships and lakes were part of Peter's everyday world. In his lifetime, he probably had fallen out of boats, jumped out of boats, or been pushed out of boats countless times, and each time he had experienced the same sinking result. But now, while his eleven friends sat shivering in the stern, Peter decided to leave his comfort zone, ignore his instincts, forget everything he'd learned from experience, and step out of the boat on Jesus' command. In the middle of a storm. At night. And the moment he realized what he'd just done, and he saw the wind and the waves, he panicked.

I understand how Peter felt after he stepped over the side of the boat and onto the tossing sea. I have felt the same heart-stopping moment of panic, that sinking feeling when you want to turn back but realize that it's much too late. After my first book was published, the leader of our church's Coffee Break Bible Study invited me to give a speech to the group. Of course I declined, assuring her that public speaking was not in my nature. I am perfectly suited to being a writer, holing up in my office for days at a time with only my imaginary characters to keep me company. Past experience in required speech classes in school had produced tearful, rubber-kneed blubbering on my part. I could not, would not, give a speech.

Then my cheerleader-friend, Cathy, heard about it. I call her a cheerleader because of her friendly, outgoing personality—the opposite of my introverted one. She is superb at encouraging the people she loves with spiritual pep talks. "You're a writer! You can easily write a speech," she gushed. Of course I can *write* a speech. It's *giving* a speech in front of real people that's the problem. It's a testimony to Cathy's powers of persuasion that I finally agreed.

I don't remember how that first speech went or what I said, but I do recall consuming fistfuls of antacids. Afterward, the Coffee Break leader quietly gave my name and phone number to other area leaders, and before long I was being asked to speak regularly. It didn't get any easier with practice. In fact, the stomach-churning, nausea-producing effects of public speaking would make an effective weight-loss plan.

Roll ahead a few years, and one day the president of the International Coffee Break organization called to ask me to be a keynote speaker at their annual convention. Again, my friend Cathy talked me into it—after I made her promise to come to the convention with me.

On the day of the speech, we went to the auditorium a few hours ahead of time so the stage crew could run a sound check. Cathy watched from the wings as I walked out onto the stage and stood at the podium. I looked out into the theater, beyond the glow of the stage lights, and saw row after row of empty seats. Not dozens or hundreds of seats but thousands of them. I imagined them filled with people in a few hours and my knees went weak. The spotlights began to spin. If I hadn't gripped the podium I would have fallen over. I couldn't do this! I couldn't speak before an audience of more than two thousand people. What was I doing here? Why had I ever agreed to speak? I understood exactly how Peter must have felt after he stepped over the side of the boat.

"*Lynn!*" A booming voice called to me out of the darkness. I hoped it was the voice of God, calling me home to heaven, but it wasn't. "Lynn, could you please say something so we can check the microphone levels?"

How could I speak? My lungs felt as if I'd fallen from a tree and had the wind knocked out of me. Cheerleader Cathy hurried over with the Bible she carries in her purse and pushed it into my shaking hands. "Here, read something," she whispered. I opened it at random, drew an asthmatic breath, and began to read from the Psalms. It helped to be looking down at the page instead of out at the endless rows of seats. The familiar words of Scripture eased my panic long enough to finish the sound check. But reading in an empty auditorium was one thing—how would I ever deliver a speech before a packed house later tonight? I was in over my head and about to drown. I had come close to drowning once before in Tilson Lake when I was in the eighth grade. The breathless, heart-stopping panic I experienced back then had felt exactly like this. Unless God performed a miracle, I couldn't possibly walk out onto this stage in a few hours and give a coherent speech.

When the sound check ended, Cathy grabbed my arm and towed me back to our hotel room. She closed the door and pulled me to my knees beside one of the beds, saying "We need to pray!" Cathy did all the praying. I was too incoherent with fear to utter a sound.

The next few hours passed in a blur. We dressed for the event, went to dinner with the organizers—although I couldn't eat a bite of it—and returned to the auditorium for the program. "I'll be praying," Cathy said as she left me to take her seat in the audience. I felt as though I was drowning again as the leaders escorted me to a room backstage to pray with me. I didn't hear a word they said. With my mind whirling and my pulse throbbing in my ears, I silently cried out to God, the same way I had cried out to my friends on the shore of Tilson Lake: "Help! Help me!"

Months before, I had asked God if He was calling me to give this speech, and I had felt that He was. I had stepped out of the boat at His command. But now, like Peter, I had taken my eyes off Jesus to look around at my circumstances, and I was sinking fast. It would take a miracle just to be able to stand upright and draw a breath, let alone speak. And so, like Peter, I cried out, "Lord, save me!"

I always found it strange that when Peter began to sink he didn't try to swim back to the boat. We know from Scripture that he could swim. After Jesus' resurrection, Peter jumped out of a boat and swam to shore when he saw Jesus cooking breakfast on the beach. But instead of doing the dog paddle and trying to save himself, Peter cried out to Jesus. I love the next word in the story: *immediately.* "Immediately Jesus reached out his hand and caught him" (Matthew 14:31).

And in the hushed room backstage that night, I cried out for help and *immediately* . . . the sound of a shofar pierced the quiet. The trumpeting came from everywhere and nowhere, echoing throughout the auditorium. *A shofar!* God had chosen His response especially for me. Never mind that in real life the music came from a rabbi onstage who had been hired to play the opening trumpet call for the entire convention. Never mind that everyone, not just me, could hear it. God had chosen the perfect symbol to speak to me—and only me—in that moment.

My husband is a professional trumpet player, so I know the rich history of the shofar, fashioned from a ram's horn. As Abraham prepared to sacrifice his son Isaac, foreshadowing Christ's sacrifice, Isaac asked, "Father . . . where is the lamb for the burnt offering?" Abraham answered, "God himself will provide the lamb for the burnt offering, my son" (Genesis 22:7–8). And God provided a ram that day, caught in a thicket by its horns—and He provided His own Son, Jesus Christ, to die in our place. When used in Jewish worship, the sound of a ram's horn is a reminder that the Lord will provide salvation.

Backstage, I heard the shofar sounding on and on. I bowed my head, scarcely breathing as the call gripped me like no other response from God could have. It was so loud, so penetrating and commanding, that the women stopped praying aloud. The sound shivered through me. *The Lord will provide.* In that holy moment, I felt a profound sense of peace. I knew that God would help me do what was impossible to do on my own.

The trumpet call finally ended and died away. My hands had stopped trembling. My breathing and heart rate had returned to normal. When I stood, my legs held me. I walked onto the stage—walking on water—and allowed God to use me to deliver that speech.

I've always believed that Peter became the leader of the disciples because of what he'd experienced during that midnight storm. From that night on, he knew that if he stepped out of his comfort zone at the Lord's call, he could do the impossible. He could walk on water. It was a lesson that the other eleven disciples, remaining safely in the boat, hadn't learned. And I had learned it, too, on the night of that speech. God is reminding me of that night as I look out at the stormy Sea of Galilee. Jesus will help me through all the changes and challenges I face. He'll help me walk on water if I ask for His help and reach for His hand.

The storm over the Sea of Galilee has exhausted itself. We finally step outside our vehicle again as the rain stops. The wind dies down to a gentle breeze as if stilled by Jesus' command. I see people pointing to the sky and I look up; in place of the black storm clouds, a rainbow now appears in the sky above the water. It seems laughable, a cliché, but we snap photographs of it just the same. It's a stunning symbol of God's promise: No matter how justified His wrath against mankind, His grace always shines brighter.

Before I came on this pilgrimage, the storm clouds had been building back home. My boat was rocking, my fear building. I've been hanging on to the gunwales, begging Jesus to calm the seas for me and take me back to the safety of the shore. But maybe Jesus is approaching in the storm and inviting me to walk on water in a new way, beckoning me to a deeper level of trust and faith. Am I willing to take that step, at my age, after I've reached a comfortable place in my ministry of writing and speaking? Is what I'm doing *for* Jesus something that I can easily do *without* His help? Do I dare to accept His invitation once again and step out onto the tossing waves?

> Now to him who is able to do immeasurably more than all we ask or imagine, according to his power that is at work within us, to him be glory in the church and in Christ Jesus throughout all generations, for ever and ever! Amen.

Ephesians 3:20–21

A New Prayer for the Journey

My gracious heavenly Father,
You created the wind and the waves, and You are sovereign over all of the storms in our lives. You shine the light of Your mercy on us, as brightly and as hope-filled as a rainbow after a storm. Forgive me for all the times I have failed to reflect Your light; for allowing busyness or selfishness or anything else to come before Your priority here on earth—the people You love. I confess that I have tried to blend in with the culture instead of standing out and standing up for You. I have allowed an outward standard of rules and commandments to

convince me that I'm good enough instead of allowing Christ to transform me on the inside. Thank You for giving me a second chance when I fail—and a third and a fourth chance. Give me the faith and the courage to stand up in my rocking boat on this stormy sea, and to dare to walk on water at Your invitation.

Amen

10

THE FAR NORTH

We have heard with our ears, O God; our fathers have told us what you did in their days, in days long ago. With your hand you drove out the nations and planted our fathers; you crushed the peoples and made our fathers flourish . . . for you loved them.

Psalm 44:1–3

As soon as we pull into the Dan Nature Preserve, twenty-five miles north of the Sea of Galilee, I jump off the bus, eager to begin hiking in these lush, green woods. What a contrast to the harsh, barren wilderness in the south where my journey began! This park bubbles and surges with cool, refreshing water, flowing down from the snowy slopes of nearby Mount Hermon. The water eventually joins other tributaries, like exuberant friends gathering for a party, and they become the headwaters of the Jordan River. The water continues south to the Sea of Galilee, flows down through the Jordan Valley, and eventually reaches a dead end in the Dead Sea. But here in the nature preserve the water is like a living thing as it rushes over rocks and cascades over falls, gurgling and singing and roaring with joy. It is a glorious sound that I never grow tired of hearing. The life-giving water turns the park into a veritable Eden. In fact, one leafy glade in the forest is called "Paradise," and we follow the trail markers that point the way to Paradise as we hike. To a forest-lover like me, this truly is paradise!

Long before I've had my fill of nature, we reach a stunning set of ruins that leave me speechless. Tucked away in the woods are the remains of the ancient Canaanite city of Dan, dating from the time of Abraham. The mud-brick gateway to the city is the earliest structure of its kind ever discovered, built two thousand years before Christ. I stand still, staring at the crumbling brick archway in front of me, unable to comprehend that this remnant of a man-made city is *four thousand* years old!

Genesis 14 tells the story of how Abraham's nephew Lot, who had been living among the pagans in Sodom, was captured and carried off by four kings who invaded the region. "When Abram heard that his relative had been taken captive, he called out the 318 trained men born in his household and went in pursuit as far as Dan" (v. 14). Abraham came to this Canaanite city in front of me. After a daring nighttime raid, he defeated the four kings and rescued Lot, along with all of the other captives.

I stare at this ancient archway and picture the patriarch and his weary but jubilant men marching through the gate in victory. Abraham had relied on God, not on his own strength. With only a small band of men, he had fought against an alliance of four kings, taking a daring risk to rescue a family member who should have known better than to live in the wicked city of Sodom in the first place.

We continue hiking up the hill, deeper into the woods, and arrive, breathless, at an entirely different set of ruins. Here at the top of the mountain above the ancient city of Dan are the remains of a "high place" used for idol worship. A few hundred years after Abraham, during the time of the Judges, the Israelites conquered the Canaanite city of Dan down the hill from me and set up an idol here on this high place (see Judges 17–18). The place to worship the God of Abraham was at the tabernacle in Shiloh. But this was an era when "another generation grew up, who knew neither the Lord nor what he had done for Israel" (Judges 2:10). Living among the people and cultures that they had failed to completely destroy, "they took [the pagans'] daughters in marriage and gave their own daughters to their sons, and served their gods" (Judges 3:6). The parents of these idolaters had witnessed God's powerful miracles: kingdoms conquered, walls toppled, enemies routed. Yet by the time the next generation grew up, "Everyone did as he saw fit" in his own eyes (Judges 17:6). Their forefathers' faith had slipped away like water into dry ground. It happens again and again, in Scripture and throughout the ages.

When David became king, he started a spiritual revival in Israel. His son Solomon built a magnificent Temple and designated Jerusalem as the place to worship God. But one generation after Solomon's death, the nation fractured in two, and the king of the northern tribes made two golden calves for his people to worship. He set up one here on this high place in Dan where I'm standing (1 Kings 12: 29–30).

Pomegranates

The people could worship this god of pleasure and sensuality without all the bother of God's demanding laws or the inconvenience of a long trip to Jerusalem. These ruins bear witness to that generation's idolatry.

The Dan Nature Preserve is a place of contrasts. The lush park makes me long for Eden and restores something vital inside me, as hiking through forests and near streams always does. But to find the remains of pagan worship in this beautiful Israeli park sobers me. From paradise to idolatry is such a short, swift fall. Lot wandered away from Abraham and ended up in Sodom. A generation after the conquest of the Promised Land, Israel's sons and daughters built this high place. A generation after King Solomon built a magnificent Temple in Jerusalem, Israelites were bowing down to a golden calf here in Dan.

How easy it is for a new generation to walk away from the God of their parents. How simple to follow a new path, never noticing how far it takes us from God, especially when it makes our lives more pleasurable and convenient. Why make the sacrifice of a long trip to Jerusalem when you can worship any way you want, close to home? Within my own lifetime, I've watched our culture drift far away from God, calling "good" evil and "evil" good. I can name beloved young people in my extended family for whom the convenience of easy morality and the lure of counterfeit gods speak louder than Scripture. Slowly, seductively, a new generation is drawn to the popular culture more than they are to God. And it seems more impossible with each passing year to fight such powerful forces.

But the ancient Canaanite gateway in the Dan Nature Preserve gives me hope. With faith in God and only a small band of men, Abraham defeated four powerful enemy kings and rescued his foolish young nephew. This idolatrous high place on the top of the hill now lies deserted, the golden calf long gone. The only reminders that a pagan culture ever flourished here are a few scattered remains of their worship area and a remnant of their mud-brick wall. In spite of the odds, evil does not win in the end. God does.

I can go to battle for my loved ones against enormous odds, knowing that God is on my side. "Through you we push back our enemies; through your name we trample our foes" (Psalm 44:5). With His help, I can rescue those who have been taken captive by our popular culture, but it does require that I love them enough to go to battle for them against powerful enemies. It might mean stepping out of my comfort zone and becoming involved in the lives of this younger generation in more meaningful ways. It might mean drawing closer to God and eliminating the idolatry from my own life first, before I can become a godly influence. It might mean earning the right to be heard through acts of love and grace.

Prayer is our greatest weapon in this battle for the hearts and minds of our loved ones, yet I have allowed my own prayer life to become stale and routine. I need to renew it for the sake of those I love, those whom God loves. And while I'm on my knees, I will pray for renewed faith and zeal as I search for ways to tell a lost generation that God loves them. And I will also ask God to forgive me for not vigorously chasing after my captured loved ones sooner, invading enemy territory with His help, and bringing God's children home to Him.

Mount Hermon

I've seen it in the distance from Galilee. On a clear day, Mount Hermon dominates the northeastern horizon, a majestic, snowy-haired king cloaked in purple. Our tour bus has climbed the mountain on a road with steep, winding switchbacks, and we're now gazing down on Galilee from above. This is about as far north as we can go and still be in Israel. From this vantage point, I see the nations of Lebanon and Syria in the distance.

The United States has an abundance of mountain ridges like this one, but the Mount Hermon range is conspicuous as the only snowcapped one in Israel. The sight of Hermon is so majestic, the view from the top so awe-inspiring, that I can't help wonder why God didn't build His Temple here. Mount Hermon could have inspired worshipers the way soaring medieval cathedrals in Europe were designed to do. Instead, God chose Mount Zion—which isn't even the tallest peak in

Jerusalem—as the mountain of the Lord. Then I remember the long, steep climb our bus just made to get here, and I realize that we would have used Hermon's height as an excuse. Who can climb more than nine thousand feet above sea level to worship? God chose to make His place of worship accessible.

Learning to worship was one of the reasons God brought Israel out of Egypt. "Let my people go," He told Pharaoh, "so that they may worship me" (Exodus 7:16). Yet when the people finally reached Mount Sinai and the mountain began to quake and heave, spewing fire and smoke, the people were terrified (Exodus 19:16–19). Moses climbed Sinai alone to receive the Torah, bringing God's words down to them. "Now what I am commanding you today is not too difficult for you or beyond your reach," he assured them. "It is not up in heaven, so that you have to ask, 'Who will ascend into heaven to get it and proclaim it to us so we may obey it?' . . . No, the word is very near you; it is in your mouth and in your heart" (Deuteronomy 30:11–12, 14).

The writer of the book of Hebrews recalls Israel's experiences at Mount Sinai and assures you and me that "You have not come to a mountain that can be touched and that is burning with fire . . . But you have come to Mount Zion, to the heavenly Jerusalem . . . to Jesus the mediator of a new covenant" (Hebrews 12:18, 22, 24). Our Christian walk isn't an impossible one. It doesn't require superhuman effort or intelligence, only trust. Christ left His throne in heaven to bring the kingdom down to us. He gave us the Holy Spirit to convict us of sin and teach us how to live righteous lives. What more do we need? This passage in Hebrews concludes with these words: "Therefore . . . let us be thankful, and so worship God acceptably with reverence and awe" (Hebrews 12:28).

Has the effortless accessibility that we have to our Father's throne made us complacent? Is that why I take it for granted, instead of seeing it for the amazing privilege that it is? Shouldn't I be as breathless with awe as I stand before God in worship or in prayer as if I had climbed a nine-thousand-foot mountain?

Our guide pulls my attention back as he tells us about Jesus' transfiguration. He's convinced that Jesus led Peter, James, and John at least partway up Mount Hermon and not to Mount Tabor, where the Church of the Transfiguration now stands. The Gospels don't name the mountain, saying only that Jesus took these three men up a high mountain by themselves. What happened next was life-changing: "There he was transfigured before them. His face shone like the sun, and his clothes became as white as the light. Just then there appeared before them Moses and Elijah, talking with Jesus" (Matthew 17:2–3).

In his excitement, Peter offered to build three booths as a shrine, but while he was still babbling, "a bright cloud enveloped them" and God's voice spoke from the cloud. The reaction of all three disciples was to fall facedown on the ground in terror. We sometimes sing silly praise songs about wanting to see God and to touch Him, but the truth is, if He did respond to such a naïve request, we would pass out from fright. During Israel's experience at Mount Sinai, "The sight was so terrifying that Moses said, 'I am trembling with fear'" (Hebrews 12:21). I don't ever want to forget that God is holy— and that I'm not. At the very least, when I come before Him in worship, I should leave all of my petty, self-centered thoughts and attitudes at the foot of the mountain and "Enter his gates with thanksgiving and his courts with praise" (Psalm 100:4).

For all three disciples, this mountaintop experience, conversing with Jesus and two of history's greatest men, was probably one of the most memorable of their lives. Up here where the air is thin and pure, the view unending, Peter could catch a far-reaching glimpse of God's plan for the tiny mortals far below. The roles that Moses the lawgiver, Elijah the prophet, and Jesus the Messiah each played must have seemed as clear as the air they breathed. No wonder Peter offered to build booths and live here.

We sometimes have a similar mountaintop experience at a spiritual retreat or a Christian conference, where we see the glory of God—and we long to linger there. Everything in our lives seems to fall into place as God speaks clearly to us, giving us a glimpse of His eternal perspective. We have the faith to move mountains and we say, like the Israelites at Mount Sinai, "We will do everything the Lord has said" (Exodus 19:8).

I believe that this vision of Christ in all His glory helped sustain the three disciples through all they endured in the years that followed Christ's ascension. They knew that they would see this Jesus again—in all His glory—at the end of time. We can also treasure the glimpses of His glory that He gives us, those daily miracles when our prayers for a sick friend are answered with healing; when our pleas for a torn relationship lead to reconciliation; when a loved one we've prayed for over the years finally surrenders to Christ. These glimpses help us hang on to the promise of a future when God will wipe away all tears and make all things new; a future in which Jesus has promised that "the righteous will shine like the sun in the kingdom of their Father" (Matthew 13:43).

As glorious as the experience of Christ's transfiguration was, He and His disciples couldn't stay on the mountaintop. Jesus had to travel the road to Calvary. Peter, James, and John had to go into all the world and make disciples. They all had work to do down below—and so do I. My pilgrimage to Israel is nearly over. I have traveled from one end of the nation to the other, from the barren wilderness in the south to Israel's highest peak in the north. I have seen my life and my work from a new perspective, and Christ has become real to me in ways I've never before experienced. But now it's time to take one last look at the panoramic view of the Promised Land from Mount Hermon's height. It's time to descend to ground level and prepare for the tasks that He has set before me. I go with a twinge of regret to be leaving a place of such beauty and the sense of God's presence. But I'm not leaving behind the nearness of God. He is accessible wherever I go, through prayer: "And surely I am with you always, to the very end of the age" (Matthew 28:20). What do I have to fear?

> I will utter hidden things, things from of old—what we have heard and known, what our fathers have told us. We will not hide them from [our] children; we will tell the next genera-tion the praiseworthy deeds of the Lord, his power, and the wonders he has done.
>
> Psalm 78:2–4

A NEW PRAYER FOR THE JOURNEY

Our holy God and Father,
Your glory shines in the beauty of Your creation, in
mountains and forests and rushing streams. They are

Your gifts to us to enjoy, a reflection of Your beauty and love, and I praise You for them. I confess that I have watched loved ones wander away from You and have not loved them enough to arm myself through prayer and chase after them. Give me renewed faith and zeal and the Holy Spirit's guidance as I set out to reclaim them for You. Thank You for reaching down from the heavens to rescue me so that I could be lifted up to the heavenly places with You. And now, Lord, I'm beginning to see the work You have for me to do next. Strengthen me with Your power and Your love to get it done.

Amen

11

SABBATH REST

Come to me, all you who are weary and burdened, and I will
give you rest.

Matthew 11:28

It's Friday afternoon, and the Sabbath is coming. We have
returned to the guesthouse in Jerusalem, and I'm watching
the flurry of activity that precedes this day of rest. The Hebrew word for Sabbath—*Shabbat*—means to stop. And when
the sun sets today at 4:47 p.m., all work will cease whether it's
finished or not. The public buses will all return to the station
and cease running. In homes and apartments all over Jerusalem,
people will turn off their televisions and computers and cell
phones, they'll stop checking their email and text messages.
Right now the chefs in our guesthouse kitchen are racing to
finish our special Shabbat meal, knowing that the stoves and
ovens must be turned off before sunset, whether the food is
cooked or not. I've been assured that our meal will be done.

The Jewish people have been celebrating Shabbat for centuries, in cities and villages, in ghettos and gulags and concentration camps. They know how to keep the Sabbath. As I celebrate it with them here in Israel, I'm learning to see it the way they do: as a gift from God. He gives us permission to stop working, whether we're finished or not—and of course we're never finished. We can lay down our saws and spatulas and cell phones, turn off our cars and computers and calculators, and rest. Just as our bosses and CEOs give us a yearly vacation, letting us leave work and not worry about returning tomorrow to punch a time clock or empty our in-box, God gives us a vacation from our labor every week on the Sabbath. Since He designed us and formed us, He knows that after six days our bodies and minds need to rest in order to function well—just as regular, scheduled oil changes keep our cars running at peak performance.

As sunset nears, everyone in our tour group puts on their nicest clothes. People dressed up this way for church on Sunday when I was a girl. My sisters and I even had special shoes that we wore only on that day, black patent leather ones that we polished with Vaseline on Saturday night until they gleamed. Dressing up for Shabbat is a way to set this day apart as a special, sacred time, different from all other days.

We make our way across the courtyard to the dining hall, and I'm struck by how quiet it is outside. There's no traffic in the streets, no jangling phones or beeping text messages, no music or televisions blaring from open windows. The peace is glorious, a foretaste of heaven's peace. A lot of people I know are going to feel restless and uncomfortable in heaven because they haven't practiced resting here on earth. I imagine them unable to relax in paradise as they search for a computer to access their social media, their fingers itching for a cell phone so they can send a text message. I don't want to be one of them.

Inside the dining room the tables have been set with white tablecloths and napkins, the best china and flatware, and decorated with flowers and candles. "Remember the Sabbath day and keep it holy," God commanded. *Holy* means "set apart," "dedicated to the service of God." These special dinner preparations help separate God's day from ordinary days. On ordinary days we eat take-out food on the run or meals reheated in the microwave. We shop for groceries and do laundry and mow the lawn. On ordinary days we multitask in a continual frenzy of activity before falling into bed, exhausted. But on the Sabbath, we don't have to do any of those things. This isn't legalism; it's a gift from God. It's freedom. "Remember that you were slaves in Egypt and that the Lord your God brought you out of there. . . . Therefore the Lord your God has commanded you to observe the Sabbath day" (Deuteronomy 5:15). Who wants to be enslaved again, browbeaten by taskmasters? For one day out of seven, God frees us from the tyranny of work.

Our daughter, Maya, has joined us for Shabbat, and we sit down together to eat a long, leisurely meal. She gushes with excitement as she tells us about her studies here in Jerusalem, and her joy is contagious. I can see the deep love that she has for the Jewish people, for their faith and their traditions, and I know it is God-given. After our host recites the blessing over the traditional Challah bread, Maya explains that Jewish women always bake two loaves on Shabbat. They do it to remember the manna they ate in the wilderness and how, unlike on ordinary days, God provided enough manna on the eve of the Sabbath to last for two days. The people could rest, even in the wilderness, knowing that for one full day no one had to labor to gather their daily bread, knowing that God had provided for their needs.

Our meal proceeds with prayers of thanksgiving, with laughter and an occasional song. Freed from the rush of our busy lives, we take time to really taste the food and wine, to enjoy and savor the many flavors. And also to enjoy each other. The Sabbath is a day for inviting friends and guests to share your meal, to talk face-to-face, to laugh and sing and thank God for life and for friendship. This is what we were created for. "It is not good for the man to be alone," God told us, even in the paradise of Eden (Genesis 2:18).

Of course, keeping the Sabbath is very inconvenient in our modern culture. It makes no sense at all, economically or practically, to set aside our endless work for twenty-four hours. Our in-boxes would overflow with email, our phones would be jammed with voice messages and texts. We live as though it's up to us to keep the wheels of the universe in motion, as if our work is more important than honoring God. "Sunday is my only day to shop or do laundry or clean the house," I hear people say. And so we shove God into one hour a week—unless the kids have a soccer game, and then we'll have to miss church altogether. Some churches have Saturday night services for our convenience, so we can shoehorn God into our busy weekend schedules. A day that's completely devoted to God can be very impractical.

What I'm learning here is that devout Jews honor God by rearranging their weekly schedules around Shabbat, planning for it ahead of time as if preparing for an honored guest. The cupboards are full, the food is all cooked and ready to enjoy for the next twenty-four hours, the house and the children have been scrubbed and cleaned and put in order. With everything ready, the people can offer this day and themselves to God—and to each other. And when the sun sets again at the close of Shabbat, they'll be refreshed and replenished, ready for another week of work.

Christians seem to have an aversion to anything that smacks of legalism. Didn't Christ say that the Sabbath was made for man, not man for the Sabbath? (Mark 2:27). But I can't escape the simple fact that observing the Sabbath is also one of the Ten Commandments. We remember the Sabbath because God "rested on the seventh day. Therefore the Lord blessed the Sabbath day and made it holy"—different, set apart from all the other days (Exodus 20:11). And we rest because He delivered His people out of slavery to their work in Egypt. Whether it makes sense or not, whether it's convenient or not, the Jewish people rest out of obedience, as a way to love God with all their heart and soul and mind and strength.

My daughter and I laugh as we remember her frustration growing up because I wouldn't let her go to the mall on Sunday. I suppose it was a holdover from my own youth when stores were closed on Sunday. I wanted to have at least one way to honor the Sabbath and make it different—and so our family doesn't shop on that day. We don't clean the house or mow the lawn or do laundry. I turn off my computer and close the door to my office. Now my daughter finally understands why, and in one of those rare moments that parents only dream about, she thanks me for it.

Our dinner concludes with a sumptuous dessert. Shabbat is a day to "Taste and see that the Lord is good" (Psalm 34:8), not to count calories. As we sing one final song, my musician husband reminds us that *rest* is also a musical term.

Without rests, music would become tiresome, the performers and audience exhausted. Moments of rest give music its rhythm—and so it is with Sabbath rest. Taking time from our busy, frantic lives to rest and honor God helps us restore the healthy rhythm and balance that God modeled when He rested from His own work on the seventh day.

On the Sabbath we remember to rest *on* God, trusting Him for all of our practical needs such as our daily bread and for strength in our trials. The Sabbath helps us remember to rest *in* God, trusting Him for our salvation, knowing that none of the work we do will ever gain us entrance into heaven. And it helps us remember to rest *for* God, because when we organize our lives and our work around a special day to honor Him, He is glorified. Can you imagine what a witness we would be to a restless, exhausted world if Christians set apart the Sabbath as holy, making it different from our ordinary days?

The night has grown late. We push back our chairs, reluctant to leave this bountiful table, sad to see the evening come to an end. Our host blesses God, thanking Him for our dinner and for the warm fellowship we have shared. We wish each other "Shabbat Shalom"—Sabbath peace and rest. Then the evening meal ends, and the Sabbath day continues with Jesus' invitation to us in Matthew 11:28: "Are you tired? Worn out? Burned out on religion? Come to me. Get away with me and you'll recover your life. I'll show you how to take a real rest" (THE MESSAGE).

Morning Praise

It's Saturday morning, and the city of Jerusalem is still quiet. No public buses clog the streets; no rushing, honking cars disturb the peace. Since Jews count their days from sunset to sunset, today is still the Sabbath, a day of rest and worship. From the balcony of our guesthouse in the Old City, I watch a steady stream of Orthodox men in their furry Sabbath hats going to the Kotel—the Wall—to pray.

Our tour guide has returned home to spend Shabbat with his family, but before leaving, he suggested a few sites that our group might want to visit on our own today. I set out with my husband and a few others to see the Tower of David nearby, but as I'm walking I can't shake the feeling that there is something else I need to do instead. My mind can't possibly absorb any more information, and what I really need is time to sit quietly and pray as I ponder all of the things I've already heard and seen. I turn around and walk back toward our room, alone.

As I slip through the gate and enter the courtyard to our guesthouse, I'm halted by the sound of voices and instruments lifted in glorious praise. It's coming from Christ Church, which is on the grounds of the guesthouse where we've been staying. According to the sign out front, Christ Church is the oldest Protestant church in the Middle East. This morning a Messianic Hebrew congregation is worshiping there. I feel a huge nudge—*this* is where I'm supposed to be today. I'm drawn up the steps and through the church doors as if pulled by ropes. A friendly usher gives me a set of headphones to hear the English translation since the service is in Hebrew, then he leads me to an empty pew. I don't need to use the headphones to join the singing because the Hebrew lyrics are translated into English on the screen up front and God understands every language.

For the next forty minutes, I'm engulfed in worship. I can't stop my tears as I sing and praise God. Nearly all of the words are from the Psalms, and they seem meant for me alone, balm for my heart after saying good-bye to my daughter last night. I thought my mother-heart would break as I held her tightly, wishing I didn't have to let her go again so soon. Now, as my *hallelujahs* join the others filling the church, I discover that my grief has eased as I've taken my mind off myself for a few minutes and turned my thoughts to God. Yes, this is where He wanted me to be this morning.

St. Steven's Church, Jerusalem

Much too soon the stirring praise service ends, and we take our seats. I put on the headphones and hear the minister announce that a baby girl is going to be baptized now. As the young couple steps forward with their tiny daughter, a fresh stab of pain knifes my heart. My arms feel empty all over again. I want to leave, but the pew has filled during the praise service, and I would have to tromp over everyone to escape. I'm trapped, forced to stay and listen.

"This isn't an ordinary baptism," the minister begins. He is beaming, as if unable to contain his joy. "I want everyone to know that this child is a miracle! An answer to prayer!" He explains how the young mother was unable to have children for seven long, painful years—and suddenly he is telling my story. I also struggled through seven endless years of waiting, unable to get pregnant. I remember my heartache and confusion as I wrestled to understand why God wasn't answering my prayers. But then He did answer them, and like this couple, I was finally blessed with a child—my son Benjamin. Twenty-two months later, God gave me an additional blessing—my daughter, Maya.

At the time, a friend who shared my joy said, "These children are your very own 'Samuels,'" referring to the man of God from Scripture whose barren mother, Hannah, had begged God for a child. Hannah's words of joy and thanksgiving became my own when I dedicated both of my children to God. And now the minister was reading those very words as he prepared to baptize this little girl: "I prayed for this child, and the Lord has granted me what I asked of him. So now I give him to the Lord. For his whole life he will be given over to the Lord" (1 Samuel 1:27–28).

I am weeping so hard that the woman next to me hands me a tissue. She briefly squeezes my hand, and I smile to reassure her that I'm okay. But I am overwhelmed by the goodness and love of God in bringing me here today and speaking to my heart in such a powerful way. I silently praise Him for reminding me that Benjamin may be far from home, but his studies will prepare him to serve God. And Maya's studies here in Israel will prepare her for her work among the Jewish people. I recall her joy and excitement as we talked last night, how thrilled she was to finally be realizing her dream. I see how faithful God has been in the lives of my two "Samuels," and I offer them up to Him once again to follow their callings.

I bow my head and ask God to forgive me for selfishly wanting anything for my children other than what He wants. And then, as I watch this beautiful baby girl being baptized, God's peace floods through me. Like Hannah and this new mother, I prayed for a child, and the Lord graciously gave me what I asked for—in fact, He gave me more than I asked for. And now I give my children back to the Lord. For as long as they live, they belong to Him. And nobody can snatch them from His hand.

Evening Worship

After the sun sets, ending this day of Sabbath rest, the city of Jerusalem revs up again. We walk to the Kotel and find it bustling with people enjoying the beautiful evening with their families. Hundreds of earnest worshipers are praying at the Wall—Orthodox men in black hats and striped prayer shawls alongside young people in blue jeans and uniformed soldiers with guns. What draws them here tonight?

The Kotel is unlike any place of worship I have ever visited. There are a dozen scattered plastic chairs to sit on, but they aren't aligned in neat rows as in Christian churches. A song might erupt here or there, but nothing is planned. No one passes out church bulletins, no formal liturgy is scheduled. There are no pipe organs or PowerPoint screens or praise bands. In fact, there isn't even a building in which to worship, only this open-air plaza and a remnant of the two-thousand-year-old retaining wall that once surrounded the Temple Mount. These worshipers have only the Scriptures, each other, and God, yet I'm very aware that worship is taking place here. There is a tangible sense of awe and a belief in what cannot be seen. By faith, these murmured prayers, whispered beneath prayer shawls or tucked into the wall's overflowing cracks, are going somewhere. A compassionate and loving God is listening. He hears.

Worship at the Kotel is stripped of all the symbols and traditions that I'm accustomed to, and I find that my expectations of what a worship service should be are shattered, my motives for attending laid bare. No wonder my worship times back home have seemed as dry and stale as last year's saltines. Here I see that the goal of gathering at a place of worship isn't to digest a meal that satisfies all my personal tastes, leaving me contented and filled. Nor is worship a spiritual vitamin supplement that I can gulp down to energize me for a busy week. Meeting with God is more like an appointment at the vision center to get my glasses adjusted—and maybe finding out that I need a new prescription altogether. My daily quiet time isn't an item to check off on a to-do list but an appointment with The Boss to get my priorities realigned and a new assignment to complete. I'm a soldier reporting to her Commanding Officer for updated battle plans. I need to be quiet and listen.

True worship means setting my gaze on God and the beauty of His holiness, not on myself and my needs as if God were a heavenly vending machine, dispensing answers to my prayers. It would be a terrible thing to attend weekly church services as if stuffing my requests between the stones of the Kotel, and then walking away without taking time to stand before God in silence and asking what He wants for me and from me. Worship should remind me of who God is and who I am, and what I am called to do and to be. The result of worship on my part is to say yes to the assignment I've been given and recommit to becoming the person God created me to be. My praise should flow not only because He answered a specific prayer but because every day His mercies are new. His grace alone could keep me praising until dawn.

Why come here, to a rugged remnant of an ancient retaining wall? I believe these men and women come to the Kotel because there is a sense of God's presence here and also a feeling of solidarity. All types of Jews, from the Orthodox to those in army fatigues, worship here. They pray the same psalms, recite the same Scriptures, worship the same God. As individuals, they will leave this place and pursue different courses in life, but for a few precious moments of worship, they are together as God's people, worshiping separately yet together.

And that's another lesson I learn here. Worship is private, yet corporate. God sees us as individuals, yet also as part of His body, just as each Jew is an individual and yet a member of the family of Abraham. Even though no one organizes the worshipers at the Wall and says, "Let's sing this hymn or pray this prayer," these men and women are united in their worship, an exhibit for the world to see by their survival and their continued faith in the God of Abraham. I look at them and praise God for His faithfulness to His Word: "I will surely gather them from all the lands where I banish them in my furious anger and great wrath; I will bring them back to this place and let them live in safety. They will be my people, and I will be their God. I will give them singleness of heart and action, so that they will always fear me for their own good and the good of their children after them" (Jeremiah 32:37–39). His faithfulness to them reassures me of His continued faithfulness to me.

When the body of Christ worships together, we serve as a witness, as well. That's what Jesus prayed for on the night He was betrayed: "I pray also for those who will believe in me through [the disciples'] message, that all of them may be one, Father, just as you are in me and I am in you. May they also be in us so that the world may believe that you have sent me" (John 17:20–21). We need each other. We need the solidarity of worshiping together as one.

I want to take this example of worship at the Kotel home with me and remember that the church is more than a beautifully decorated building with everyone acting and talking and thinking alike. It's more than a particular liturgy or style of music or inspiring sermons. Christ's worshiping church is a group of people from every tribe and nation and language, standing as one to worship, then returning to the daily tasks He has given us, trusting in His power, acting in His love.

The Kotel and its open-air plaza bear no resemblance to an inspiring cathedral or a modern mega-church. It's nothing but a fragment of a wall, an ancient ruin. A pitiful remnant of a once-glorious Temple with its golden roof, acres of courtyards, and gleaming vessels of gold and silver; with priests in embroidered robes, the scent of incense and roasting meat filling the air, and choirs of Levites singing praises to God. What remains is a crumbling fragment of that glory. But circumstances and loss can't stop these worshipers from coming to the Kotel on a warm winter evening and expressing their love and praise. I join them, my heart overflowing with gratitude.

> Though the fig tree does not bud and there are no grapes on the vines, though the olive crop fails and the fields produce no food, though there are no sheep in the pen and no cattle in the stalls, yet I will rejoice in the Lord, I will be joyful in God my Savior.
>
> Habakkuk 3:17–18

A NEW PRAYER FOR THE JOURNEY

My loving heavenly Father,

You created the universe in wisdom and love, and then crowned Your workmanship with rest. In Christ this world is held together, not by my puny labors and efforts. Forgive me for refusing Your gift of rest, for foolishly thinking that my work and my agenda are more important than Your command to stop and keep this day holy for You. Thank You for worship, for a chance to join with the body of Christ to praise You for Your goodness, a chance to stop and listen for Your voice. Thank You for my children and for reminding me that they aren't mine but Yours. Help me to entrust them to Your care. And help me to rest in You for my salvation; to rest on You for my daily bread; and to rest from all of my own labors for Your glory.

Amen

12

GOING HOME

Therefore, since we are surrounded by such a great cloud of witnesses, let us throw off everything that hinders and the sin that so easily entangles, and let us run with perseverance the race marked out for us.

Hebrews 12:1

I'm sitting in the departure lounge at Ben Gurion Airport, preparing to leave Israel and fly home. My journal is crammed with notes to digest, my camera bursting with photographs. Yet the picture that sticks in my mind is of something I saw on my Sabbath walk in Jerusalem yesterday afternoon. I stopped to peer through a hole in a construction fence at a new building going up. The workers began by digging a deep foundation—and of course they encountered ancient ruins and artifacts just below the surface. Sandbags and a grid of excavation pits marked the archeological dig site. But I could tell by the piles of building materials, cranes, and bulldozers parked all over the vacant lot that the construction was moving forward even as the archaeologists continued to examine and record the past. I pulled my head out of the viewing hole and studied the poster emblazoned across the construction fence, the architect's vision of the finished building. Past, present, and future collided right before my eyes.

Time seems to compress here in Israel. Like that construction site, this trip enabled me to envision the past, the present, and the future all at once—a God's-eye view of time. The past is visible in the ancient ruins I've seen, reminding me that the roots of my faith go very deep. All of the stories and people in the Bible, all of the events recorded there, have shaped my faith and provided a foundation for my life and work. But now I have to do my part and build on the foundation that has been laid. I no longer want to study the Bible as simply the record of God's work in the past, but to see that my daily sorrows and triumphs are all being added to its pages. The story of God's love for the people on planet Earth didn't stop with the book of Acts. The daily choices I make, the battles I fight, are as important as the choices and battles in the Bible.

My day-to-day work doesn't seem very glamorous: tasks equivalent to lifting heavy stones, setting beams in place, soldering pipes, and untangling wires—all according to the Architect's plans. But I still need to show up for work, putting my faith into action. Even in those painful times when it seems as though the wrecking ball is doing more tearing down than building up, God is still constructing His kingdom. He is able to use all the invisible, menial, trivial tasks I do as His construction materials.

And what about the future kingdom that God is building, that poster on the construction fence? Judging by the plans that the Architect has allowed me to glimpse in Scripture, it will be beyond my wildest imagination. The apostle John caught sight of it and wrote, "The kingdom of the world has become the kingdom of our Lord and of his Christ, and he will reign for ever and ever" (Revelation 11:15). As His workers, we can't always see the details of all the plans for the finished building. But we can bend to the task that He gives us each day, knowing that our day-to-day work matters. He makes no distinction between secular and sacred work. We build in hope and faith, believing in what we cannot see, trusting in the Master's plan.

In the meantime, the view through the construction fence challenges me to get to work, using the time and the talents that God has given me to build for His glory.

Our flight is boarding. In a flurry of activity, we collect our coats and bags and carry-ons to shuffle up the ramp and onto the airplane. Once I've stuffed, stashed, and shoved all of my belongings into place, I sink down in my seat to wait some more. I hate leaving the warm, golden sunlight and spiky palm trees of Israel for cold, snowy Chicago, but whether I like it or not, life brings change.

I see now that the purpose of this pilgrimage wasn't to give me a mystical, feel-good experience of God but to shake me out of my complacency and downright laziness, to prepare me for what He has in store for me. But before I can change the way I've been living, I need to repent and change the way I've been thinking. The Hebrew word for repentance means turning around and going in a completely different direction. It means sweeping away all of my old ways of seeing and thinking and acting, and then carefully, prayerfully replacing them with new ones. For me, it means trying to look at this stage of my life the way that God does, not the way I've been viewing it. In other words, I need to prepare for more change.

Maybe the uneasiness I've been experiencing at home can be compared to a plant that has become root-bound, forced to live in a pot that's much too small. Even though the plant has flourished and flowered and borne fruit in the past, it needs to be moved to a larger pot or it will eventually stop growing. The transplanting process is a shock, causing the plant to wilt and pout for a few days after being ripped out of its accustomed place. But soon the roots discover that they have room to grow and stretch, and before long, the tired, worn-out plant begins to send out new shoots, then it blossoms and bears fruit. God wants me to be fruitful. I need a larger pot.

Change is such a huge part of life that we should be used to it by now. Instead, we resist. We're tearful on the first day of kindergarten, fearful on the first day of high school, overwhelmed as we start college. A new job, a new spouse, a new baby—all of these changes are regular parts of a normal life, yet each of these milestones inaugurates enormous changes. God doesn't believe in retirement—not in the way I've always pictured it, baking cookies and reading stories to my grandchildren and sitting in my comfortable church pew on Sunday. So the question is, am I willing to leave the comfortable, familiar pot where I'm currently languishing and trust God to transplant me to a new one?

Imagine the enormous changes that took place in the lives of Sarah and Abraham when God transplanted them. And how everything changed again after Isaac was born to them at

Jerusalem University College

the ages of ninety and one hundred. And what about Noah? We aren't told what he did during the early years of his life, but God gave him the new ministry of ark-building at the age of five hundred. Joshua and Caleb began conquering kingdoms at the age of eighty-five. But I probably resemble Moses the most. He seemed quite comfortable tending his sheep at the age of eighty, his family gathered around him—until God stuck a burning bush in his path. Fortunately for all of us, Moses stepped forward to see what this new change was all about, and after some vigorous arguing with God—something I seem to be very good at—Moses moved to a bigger pot and accepted his calling to lead God's people out of slavery in Egypt. All of these Old Testament people accepted God's invitation to walk away from their settled, comfortable lives and begin again.

Just because I have a successful ministry doesn't mean that God doesn't have something more—or different—in my future. Little by little, life in the same old pot is killing me, causing my spiritual walk to shrivel and wither. Change will be good for me, not something to fear. It will strip away my self-sufficiency and self-reliance and force me to lean on God, to pray more, to trust Him, and to walk in faith with the One who invented change.

Our jet rumbles slowly forward and moves onto the runway—then, after a suspenseful pause, we roar down the tarmac and lift into the air. My stomach does a little flip during that brief weightless moment when the wheels leave the ground. It takes a lot of fuel, a lot of horsepower to propel this huge aircraft into the air and keep it aloft. And it took this trip—and the power of the Holy Spirit—to lift me off the ground and propel me forward.

I remember teaching our son Ben to walk when he was a baby. He was a quiet, placid child, content to either sit in one place or wait for someone to pick him up and carry him someplace new. He didn't even try to crawl very far. But Ken and I wanted more for our son than a stunted, baby life, and so we stood him on his feet—ignoring his unhappy protests—and encouraged him to start moving forward. At first we held his hands firmly in ours to keep him from falling. But we knew we couldn't hold his hands his entire life, so eventually we let go and moved a little distance away, coaxing him to toddle toward us. Ben was afraid to move. He dropped down on his padded, diapered rump and wailed. Again, we stood him on his feet and moved away. Again, he cried as if to say, "Why are you so far away? Why are you leaving me on my own? I'm scared! I feel abandoned." We were never far away. We hovered nearby, making sure he was safe, ready to pick him up when he fell. But we knew that this was the best way to teach him to walk on his own.

And maybe I was like baby Ben before this trip—stuck in place, not venturing out of my comfort zone, waiting to be carried rather than risk taking a step in a new, scary direction. God felt far away at times, but the truth is, He was always near. Even if I do fall—and I surely will—He will be there to catch me, offering forgiveness and grace, picking me up so I can begin again.

It's called a walk of faith. "Leave your country, your people and your father's household and go to the land I will show you," God told Abraham (Genesis 12:1). He had no map to guide him, only God's promises of a fruitful future. Was it scary to leave his comfortable life and walk with God, not knowing exactly where He would lead? Absolutely. But Abraham's faith and his relationship with God grew with each frightening step that he took. God called Abraham "my friend," and that's what God wants with me—with us—the intimacy of trust and friendship.

And so I return home determined to stand up and walk forward with my God in faith; determined to climb out of my tiny, claustrophobic pot so I can grow and bear fruit; determined to build my assigned part of His kingdom according to the Master's plan.

My pilgrimage to Israel might have come to an end, but the next step on my journey is just beginning.

A New Prayer for the Journey

(A prayer of Moses the man of God, from Psalm 90)

"Lord, you have been our dwelling place throughout all generations. Before the mountains were born or you brought forth the earth and the world, from everlasting to everlasting you are God. . . . A thousand years in your sight are like a day that has just gone by, or like a watch in the night. . . . Teach us to number our days aright, that we may gain a heart of wisdom. . . . Satisfy us in the morning with your unfailing love, that we may sing for joy and be glad all our days. . . . May the favor of the Lord our God rest upon us; establish the work of our hands for us—yes, establish the work of our hands."
Amen

Don't Miss Lynn Austin's Biblical Fiction!

To learn more about Lynn and her books, visit lynnaustin.org.

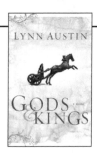
BETHANYHOUSE